*prairie***spring**

Houghton Mifflin Harcourt · *Boston · New York* · 2009

prairie spring

PETE DUNNE

Photographs by Linda Dunne

For information about permission to reproduce selections from this book,
write to Permissions, Houghton Mifflin Harcourt Publishing Company,
215 Park Avenue South, New York, New York 10003.

www.hmhbooks.com

Library of Congress Cataloging-in-Publication Data

Dunne, Pete, date.
Prairie spring / by Pete Dunne ; photographs by Linda Dunne.
p. cm.
Includes bibliographical references.
ISBN-13: 978-0-618-82220-1
ISBN-10: 0-618-82220-8
1. Prairies — North America. 2. Prairie ecology—
North America.   I. Title.
QK110.D86 2009
508.315'3097 — dc22   2008036770

Book design by Anne Chalmers
Typeface: Miller

Printed in the United States of America

DOC 10 9 8 7 6 5 4 3 2 1

Text illustrations are based on Linda Dunne's photographs.

Acknowledgments

People ask writers to identify the high point in the writing of a book. Some writers accent the day the finished manuscript is sent to the publisher; others relish the moment they tear the wraps off the "author's advanced copies."

I like this moment. The morning I sit down and reflect upon all the people who helped bring a project to fruition.

Perennials in this regard are my colleagues on the staff of the Cape May Bird Observatory and New Jersey Audubon Society. Every time I engage in one of these avocational end runs, they are the ones who must pull together and assume extra duties. They are, in sum, the finest (and most forgiving) environmental force operating under an organization banner today. In particular I need to single out Sheila Lego and Deborah Shaw, whose administrative duties are especially burdened by my absence, and my boss, New Jersey Audubon's president, Tom Gilmore, whose indulgence surpasses all known standards.

One of the best things about any writing project is the

opportunity it presents to learn. I am not, and do not pretend to be, an authority on the prairies. But I now know a good deal more than I did when Linda and I set off on this project, and for this I have many very fine writers to thank. The following authors and their works served as resources before, during, and after our travels. Many of the facts you'll find larded into this text, and not a few of the insights, originate with them. I salute them, and thank them, starting with

Candace Savage of Saskatoon, Saskatchewan, whose book *Prairie: A Natural History* ranks among the most thorough, informative, engaging, and just plain wonderfully written books treating the subject of natural history.

The *New York Times* writer Timothy Egan, whose very timely book *The Worst Hard Time* helped put the elements and hardships of this human and environmental disaster into perspective. The amazing and prolific professor emeritus of biological sciences at the University of Nebraska Paul A. Johnsgard, whose book *Prairie Dog Empire* is graduate studies and a postdoc in pure prairie ecology. And Stephen R. Jones and Ruth Carol Cushman, whose Peterson Field Guide *The North American Prairie* served as both a biological blueprint and a cook's tour guide for our travels and itinerary.

We did, of course, consult many other references during our travels and this writing, and these are listed in the bibliography. But the authors and titles just mentioned distinguished themselves as resources and as sources of inspiration.

As you will come to learn, and I hope understand, people and prairies are inexorably bound. It follows that any book focusing on the prairie environment will necessarily involve a great many people. Linda and I have many of these to thank for providing both aid and support. They include Paul and Louanne Timm, proprietors of the West Pawnee Bed and Breakfast; Brad Mellema, Bill Taddicken, Kent Scaggs, and Allison Hiff of the National Audubon Society's Rowe Sanctuary; Chana Reed of the Lamar Chamber of Commerce; Mary Breslin, editor of *The Lamar Ledger*, Tish McDaniels of The Nature Conservancy's Milnesand Preserve; Willard Hicks of the Weaver Ranch and Grasslans Foundation; and the Williamson family of Milnesand and the Known Universe.

Also Tom Peters, district ranger for the Comanche National Grassland; the biologist Beth Humphrey for the Pawnee National Grassland; Gary Brundidge, resource program manager for Custer State Park; Michael Stopps, chief ranger, Melena Stichman, biology technician, and John Doerner, chief historian for the Little Bighorn Battlefield National Monument.

My wonderful in-laws, Bob and Ann Ellis, once again provided a comfortable retreat for me to finish this writing and for Linda to go through thousands of images. Rick Radis, writer, naturalist, and friend, was generous enough to review this manuscript twice and offer valuable counsel.

And no acknowledgment in the last twenty years is or has been complete without an expression of thanks and appreciation directed toward my agent, Russ Galen of Scovil, Chichak, Galen; and my editor, Lisa White of Houghton (pronounced Ho-ton) Mifflin.

See, Lisa. I really do know how to pronounce it (even if my tongue sometimes forgets).

Contents

*prairie**spring***

PROLOGUE: *Groundhog Day*

Venus, Anpo Wicahpi to the Lakota Sioux, was bright in the eastern sky as we left our airport rental and trudged off across the snow. To the west, barely showing above the horizon, were two prominent stars, Pollux and Castor. Westerners know them as elements in the twelve-star constellation Gemini, the Twins. But to the Sioux, a people who once roamed the prairies as freely as the stars circle the sky, they are the two bright stars in the spiritually important, and seasonally significant, eight-star constellation known as the Bear's Lodge.

"Far enough," I shouted back to the Michelin Man look-alike who was my wife.

"A little farther," she replied. "Damn. The camera's viewfinder's fogging up."

No surprises there. At fifteen degrees below zero, lots of things turn truculent.

But not all.

Off in the direction of Crow Valley, a Forest Service campground on the southern border of the Pawnee National Grassland and a mile from the town of Briggsdale, Colorado (where the miniseries *Centennial* was filmed), a female great horned owl was calling. It was, aside from the squeak of snow underfoot, the only sound in the sweeping white nothingness that surrounded us. Owls are early nesters. Even here, in February, on the prairies of Colorado, the bird was probably already sitting on eggs.

"Do you hear the owl?" I asked, coming once again to a stop.

"I hear the [unspeakable, unprintable] owl," she said through a scarf so thick an alpaca might mistake her for one of its own. "But my [colorfully disparaging, sure to get edited] camera is being really cranky. It doesn't like this kind of weather at all!"

Actually, the weather was beautiful, perfect for the High Plains in winter. It was just really, really cold, which is not uncommon here, either. But books have to begin somewhere, and books whose focus is spring should begin where the season itself begins, which is deep in the season that spawns it. While some might argue that early February is jumping the gun on spring, it's really not. The angle of the sun on the second of February is the same as it is on November 10, a season our species comfortably calls "autumn" or "fall" or even "Indian summer." And if you look at a calendar, you'll note that February 2 falls halfway between December 21, the first day of winter, and March 21, the official first day of spring. To the ancient Druids, this midquarter date signaled the Imbolc celebration, a day on which animals were imbued with mystical, even prognosticating powers.

The come-out-of-your-burrow, see-your-shadow kind.

Later, the Roman Catholic Church put a sanitizing and self-serving spin on the pagan tradition with the institution of Candlemas Day—a day on which priests distributed blessed candles to ward off the winter darkness (at just about the point that winter starts turning the corner and increasing daylight is becoming obvious anyway). But the church failed to shake the holiday's superstitious foundation. Or, as the old German rhyme expresses it:

> For as the sun shines on Candlemas Day,
> So far will the snow swirl until May.
> For as the snow blows on Candlemas Day,
> So far will the sun shine before May.

It was these German immigrants who brought the Candlemas (and Groundhog) Day tradition to the United States in the 1700s.

And all this time you thought Groundhog Day was just one of those silly Hallmark card holidays, didn't you?

It's not. It has its anchoring in the earth and the sky. It is part of an earth-watching tradition handed down to us from ancient peoples who really, really understood the natural world and the seasons that circumscribe it. By their careful reckoning, Linda and I were already halfway through winter and only six weeks shy of the celestial and, perhaps, official day of spring.

Official?

Official. Modern-day Druids, and other Groundhog Day believers, were breathlessly awaiting news from Gobbler's Knob, in Punxsutawney, Pennsylvania, where the official prognosticating groundhog makes his annual proclamation. You know the legend. Maybe you've seen the pageant broadcast on the evening news, or the Bill Murray movie. Bunch of guys in top hats drag a sleep-drugged groundhog out of his den and hold him up in the air. If, as the ancient tradition has it, the groggy rodent sees his shadow, there will be six more weeks of winter, just like the Julian calendar promises. If he doesn't, we're headed for an early spring.

But Linda and I were taking no chances. Uncertain about the jurisdictional limits of a rodent that doesn't breed anywhere close to the prairies of Colorado, we'd decided to fly out and take the pulse of the season ourselves. In about ten minutes, as soon as the sun came up, we'd know how our prairie spring was progressing. Right now, judging by the golden light gathering in the eastern sky, it sure looked as though my shadow was going to take sides with the thermometer, which is to say that we could have saved ourselves a lot of airfare and stayed in our burrows back in New Jersey for another six weeks. Barring this, we could have sat in the heated seats of our airport rental parked by the side of the road and kept Linda's camera happy.

"The shadow from the car is going to get in the picture," I warned.

"Damn," said Linda, looking back, seeing it was so. "Move farther back."

"We should have come out yesterday to set up this shot," I said, none too helpfully.

"If it hadn't been snowing to beat the band, we would have," Linda shot back. "Now move a little more to the left."

"If I do that, you'll get the sign in the picture."

"I want the sign in the picture. For perspective."

"But the sign says to stay in the car in order to see wildlife. Since we're trying to encourage people to explore the prairies, we don't want to set a bad example."

There followed a few moments during which the awesome silence and unencumbered openness of the prairie landscape held sway. As a fifty-six-year-old, lifelong resident of the most densely populated state in the Union, I have come to realize that space and silence are two of the rarest and most valuable commodities on Earth. These are qualities the High Plains have in plenty. And they are only the down payment on the wonders awaiting visitors who come here.

"You are joking about the sign, right?" Linda finally asked.

"I am," I assured her.

"Good," she said, "because as far as I can see, you and I are the only living things within two time zones of here. Hold it right where you are. That's perfect."

"Uh-uh," I said, squeaking to a stop. "There was that owl before. And for all you know there could be a badger hibernating in a den right under that snowbank over there."

"Intelligent badger," Linda observed. "Bring your head up a little bit. Get ready. The sun's just touching the hilltop behind you. What are you laughing for?"

"I was just thinking how funny it would be if some officious-looking guy wearing a top hat were to reach into a hole and drag some really cranky badger out into the sunlight so it could see its shadow. Critter would probably take his arm off to the lapel of his coat."

"I thought you needed a groundhog," Linda said.

"Nope. The Druids were equal opportunity worshipers. Any old burrowing animal would do. Bears and badgers were the poster children of spring. Sad to think that nowadays, when you mention Groundhog Day, people conjure the image of Bill Murray instead of something as neat as a badger. Think we'll see any this year? I'll settle for a swift fox or a bison or two."

"Stop talking and hold still," Linda commanded. "It's happening."

"O"

It is pretty tragic when people think first of an actor playing a role, instead of an animal being itself, when considering a natural event, but it is also not uncommon—in fact, I'll go so far as to say that, for most Americans today, it is the norm. In our culture, we have largely become estranged from the natural world, make that the universe, that surrounds us. Most people are reduced to experiencing the trappings or window-dressing of the natural world instead of engaging that world itself—and they don't even know it.

Excuse me if I don't feel compelled to support this point with survey results. But I'll offer a couple of examples.

Several years ago, a West Coast resident who intended to come to Cape May to see the great concentrations of migrating shore birds and breeding horseshoe crabs, called wanting to know when the moon would be full in New Jersey.

Answer: about three hours before it's full in California. You have to allow for those pesky time zones.

While leading a tour to Kenya, I once stood with my group on the deck of a place called Mountain Lodge. It was dark. We were watching animals come down to drink at the floodlit watering hole.

"What's that?" one of the members of my tour group asked, pointing skyward.

"What's what?" I queried, seeing nothing out of the ordinary.

"That," she said again.

"What?" I asked again.

"That!" she repeated, growing exasperated. "That white stripe in the sky."

"That," I replied, trying to keep the cold, dark horror that was paralyzing my diaphragm from creeping into my voice, "is the galaxy you live in. That is the Milky Way."

About the time we started this book, there was a television ad campaign running that promoted something I could never quite comprehend except to say that it had something to do with the letter *O*, that it had nothing to do with Oprah Winfrey, and that O was something I was obviously supposed to subscribe to or buy. Anyway O (whatever it is) purported to be conversant with all facets of human endeavor: the home, the office, et cetera. To demonstrate O's command of the "outdoors" (an interest that I have a great deal of interest in), they showed an actress wearing a tennis outfit and sipping a drink through a straw.

Excuse me, but tennis does not equate to the outdoors. A tennis court is a parking lot with a net strung across it. If this is your idea of the outdoors, you have made my point by probably not understanding my point.

Tennis is a game, a human contrivance. The outdoors is the natural environment. It is as real as games are not.

But the ad did go right to the heart of the lowest (and perhaps only) common denominator linking the natural world and the millions of people who are most estranged from it. This is seasonality.

The actress in the ad was appropriately dressed for a warm-season out-of-doors activity. In the Denver airport, when Linda and I were standing in line at the car rental, we were surrounded by people heading up to the ski slopes, all wearing fleece jackets and Gore-Tex shells. They were dressed for a cold-season activity.

While people may have no familiarity with calling owls, hibernating badgers, or even the galaxy their planet is parked in, they do get the idea of seasons, and they not only recognize them but relate to them, changing their wardrobes and activity patterns to match.

Even in the heart of New York City, arguably the most environmentally estranged corner of the planet (maybe even the universe), they still change the displays in shop windows to conform to the seasons. Beach sand, clamshells, and sun-dried starfish in summer. Brightly colored leaves in autumn. Dinner plate–size snowflakes in winter.

Flowers in spring! And just as an aside, until you've seen the prairies in the spring, you only think you've seen flowers. Makes the New York garden show look like window-dressing.

So if your ambition was to write a book to entice an estranged audience to explore an exciting, overlooked, and now alien environment (i.e., the natural world that surrounds and supports them), and you were searching for some common ground to give them familiar footing, where might you start?

Please say "the seasons."

And which season would you choose?

Precisely. Consider yourself a prime candidate for adventure.

WHY HERE, WHY NOW?
Beyond the stocking cap–topped head of my wife, I could see the first piercing glint of gold peeking over the hill behind her. Something deep inside of me reached out to greet it.

I'll be honest. I don't really know what makes spring so

irresistible. But all those Romantic poets, French Impressionist painters, young lovers, old lovers, gardeners, runners, bicyclists, and people who suddenly decide to go for a lunch-hour walk the day the thermometer first tops fifty degrees are neither wrong nor misguided.

Every season has qualities that take us by the hand and invite us along. Spring grabs us by the throat.

If what I am saying makes no sense to you, if you have never felt the power of spring, then it is time for you to put this book down. Check your appointment book. You've got a tennis game at 2:00.

If what I am saying strums a chord, then what if I told you that there is a place this side of the solstice (and the Milky Way) where spring has no equal? Not a spring of grass clippings and garage sales. Not just a robin-making-a-nest-under-the-porch and tulips-coming-up-after-the-daffodils-are-done kind of spring, but half a million migrating cranes whose conjoined cries make the air tremble and your heart feel three sizes too large for your rib cage. Storm-darkened skies as black as prairie earth, and grassy plains so festooned with flowers that you look around for the Lion, the Scarecrow, the Tin Man, and Toto, too . . .

Only to discover it is not a stage set. It's real.

A place where every year, two great, eternally opposing forces vie for supremacy across an open battlefield with no less than the fate of the entire Northern Hemisphere at stake. A passion play, set on a global stage whose story is the epic struggle between light and darkness.

Lewis and Clark went exploring on this stage. John

James Audubon painted here. Custer rode to glory. Millions of American pioneers bet their lives. Fair warning: if you keep reading, you, too, may have your world turned upside down, just as the prairies were turned upside down by people who came here seeking much the same things people still seek today.

Peace. Roots. Security. Bountiful resources. Adventure. Beauty. Meaning. The secret door to all these human ambitions and more was, now, just a sunbeam's winking disclosure away.

JUST THE TWO OF US . . . MAKE THAT FOUR

Ka . . . je-e-et, Linda's camera wheezed.

Yikes, I thought but couldn't say, since I was trying to keep a smile frozen on my face. Linda's right. That camera really doesn't like this cold.

Ka . . . j-e-e-et.

"Are you sure that thing is working?" I asked. "Sounds pretty sluggish."

"Who can blame it?" she said, moving slightly to the left. Trying to get a better angle. "My feet are *freezing,* and my fingers are so numb I can hardly change the settings!"

This from a woman who used to ice-climb for a hobby and lead glacier traverses for a living.

"Try putting your arms out to your sides," she directed. "You look dumb just standing there."

"I am dumb just standing here. Like you said, we're the only things out here."

"Just you and your shadow."

"Can you see it?"

"Turn around," she invited.

Sure enough. There, stretching toward the horizon, was one long, dark six-more-weeks-of-winter-promising shadow.

Poppycock, you are thinking. Old wives' tale. Groundhog Day is a myth. Maybe so. But we in this age have lost not only intimacy with the natural world, but much of the basic wisdom our ancestors knew, too. Because there is, in fact, a basis for the groundhog and his shadow "myth," and it is grounded in mathematical probability and meteorological fact.

If the groundhog—or badger, or bear—sees its shadow, it means the sun is shining. If the sun is shining, it means clear skies. Over much of the Northern Hemisphere, including Europe, where the groundhog "myth" originated, and in North America where it was imported, clear weather in midwinter usually means cold weather—the result of cold, stable air bulging down out of the north. Warm temperatures, often resulting in cloudy skies, originate in the south.

While weather is changeable, it also commonly comes in multiple-day waves, with periods of cold weather followed by periods of warm as warm air flowing up from the south is, then, followed by cold air bulging down from the north. This is the classic spring pattern.

But in some years, the dome of high pressure that builds over Canada each winter is particularly strong, so it tends to dominate the weather pattern. The result is more days of clear, dry, cold weather than average.

A persistent Canadian high also means that, mathematically, there is a greater chance that Groundhog Day will dawn bright and sunny and the animal will see its shadow. Since weather patterns tend to be persistent, chances are therefore good that the clear, cold weather pattern that greeted the groundhog and his shadow will continue through February and into March.

The result? A late spring.

My shadow, and the odds, said the smart money was on a late spring coming to the prairies this year.

"Are we finished?" Linda wanted to know. "There's not an awful lot to shoot out here (unless you like snow). And I want to get over to Crow Valley before we lose this fantastic light."

In case you are not married to a photographer, you should know that it is always all about the light.

"Okay," I said, "but before you put your camera away, what do you say we get a picture of just my shadow? He's the star of the chapter. I don't want a picture in the book of me just standing here looking dumb."

I know I left myself wide open here, but it is a credit to Linda's professionalism, our marriage, and her ambition to get over to Crow Valley while there was still good light that she didn't say a word.

Linda moved forward. Moved left. Moved right. Stood in front of me. Lowered her camera.

"I can't get any kind of an angle," she said.

"How come?"

"Because I can't take a picture of your shadow without my shadow being in the way."

"Oh," I said. "Then show them both."

"But there might be some old Druid rule against double-teaming your prognostication. What if we get twelve more weeks of winter? That would shoot the entire project."

"Nah. I'll bet the very worst that can happen is we get disqualified from the Imbolc singles competition," I argued. "If we're challenged, I'll say you were standing in for the badger. So far, he's a no-show."

"Twelve more weeks of winter," Linda said, raising her camera. "Think about it."

I'm sure Linda was smiling behind all that alpaca, but I couldn't see it. Looking off across the frozen expanse that was the Pawnee Grassland, buried, in places, beneath several feet of wind-whipped snow, I could far more easily envision a winter extending into May than I could conceive of spring touching this corner of the planet before March.

If badgers don't come out of their burrows on February 2 in the prairies, you can bet there's a good reason for it.

Kajeet!

"Hey, our shadows kind of remind me of Pollux and Castor," I said to the shadow on my right, the one pointing the camera.

"Like the constellation?" Linda asked.

"Uh-huh. If the shot turns out, we can use it as the cover for the book! What do you think?"

There was a moment's silence that became a protracted silence that rivaled, in depth and scope, the sound of prairie in winter.

"It's perfect," I said (struggling to fill the silence). "According to Sioux mythology, Pollux and Castor are part of the constellation called the Bear's Lodge, which not only was the prairie natives' constellation for spring but is one of the celestial markers for the Race Track, in which the fate of two-legged creatures was once decided by a foot race between the four-legged creatures, who wanted us snuffed, and birds, who thought we deserved another chance."

Silence.

"Well, you have to admit, it's thematically apt. Spring. Rebirth. Second chance."

Silence.

"The birds won," I added.

"Go, birds," Linda intoned. "I'd rather have a bird on the cover than a shadow. Who was racing for our side?"

"The magpie," I answered.

Linda grimaced. "Be hard to fit a magpie on the cover," she said. "Too much tail. Was it a close race?"

"Down to the wire. Magpie hitched a ride on the back of a bison and flew ahead just at the finish line. Beat him by a bill's length."

"So he cheated," Linda said.

"Well, no," I protested. "It could be argued the magpie

was just clever. And he did save the human race. It was for a good cause."

"Don't the Sioux have any other favorite birds that might be 'thematically apt'?" she asked, hopefully.

"Well . . . yeah! There was an important demigod named Fallen Star, who was sired by a real star and born of mortal woman, then raised by a western meadowlark. The story conflates Christian teaching and ancient Roman legend, but it gets us back to Pollux and Castor, who were also raised by a wild animal—except they were suckled by a wolf, not brooded by a meadowlark."

Linda sighed. "Can't we just put a meadowlark on the cover because it's a neat-looking prairie bird?"

"Sure," I agreed. "I like meadowlarks. But," I added, looking around, "you're going to be pretty hard-pressed to get a picture of a meadowlark today. On the other hand, I'll bet all this snow cover is going to stoke a bumper crop of flowers. Could be a spring for the record books. You might want to consider putting flowers on the cover of the book, too."

"Might," Linda agreed, studying the great, white, open expanse that supported, for as far as eyes could see, nothing more than two two-legged creatures and their shadows.

Somewhere beneath the snow there were flowers waiting to emerge. Somewhere in the weeks ahead, there would be meadowlarks, and longspurs, and lark buntings, and other prairie birds throwing their forms and their songs aloft. But now it was winter. The still, white page upon which the new season would soon be written.

"Are we finished here?" Linda asked. " 'Cause if we are I still want to go over to Crow Valley. We're wasting good light."

And for the record, spring 2007 was, after all, fairly early and mild on the prairies. Our shadows, and all they portended, were wrong. As for Punxsutawney Phil, Pennsylvania's most famous groundhog, he did not see his shadow in 2007—and spring in the Northeast ran late and cold.

Yep. He was wrong, too. So much for playing the odds.

As for the promise of a bumper crop of flowers on the prairies, the answer to that question still lies many adventures and a season away, and you'll have to read on to see whether that prediction held true.

Chapter 1: March 20, 2007
Westbound into Brown

There was a great deal going on in the universe at the moment. Galaxies forming, black holes imploding, the borders of all that is and ever was expanding at a rate exceeding the speed of light (229,792,458 miles per second).

Here on planet Earth, 120 Russian coal miners were believed killed in that country's most recent mine disaster. Vice President Dick Cheney was examined by physicians after complaining of pain in his leg. Attorney General Alberto Gonzales was taking heat over the dismissal of eight, maybe nine, federal prosecutors (all of whom happened to be Democrats), and the civil efficacy of a banner promoting "Bong hits for Jesus" was being hotly debated by a lot of second parties.

While most of these matters were central to the United

States of America, a large, political construct covering the middle portion of the North American continent, there was one event due to transpire this day that had more broad-based, planetary standing. At 7:07 P.M. Central daylight-saving time, the earth would reach the halfway point in its seasonal swings between summer and winter, the equinox. In the Northern Hemisphere, the milestone would mark the end of the season winter and the onset of spring.

Just about the time we were learning about the attorney general's difficulties, Linda and I, along with our canine companions, Max and Raven, were driving west on I-74 at a fraction of the speed of the expanding universe (but still fast enough to draw the ire of a particularly mean-spirited state trooper). Traffic was light. We'd cleared Indianapolis just ahead of morning rush hour, and it was still too early in the season for "snowbirds" to be heading home in their RVs.

Us? We were en route to Kearney, Nebraska, hoping to catch up with half a million northbound sandhill cranes, who were, themselves, responding to a seasonal swing all their own called "migration."

But northbound or westbound, eastbound or just standing still, it doesn't make much difference where you are or what you are doing insofar as the timing of the seasons go. Whether you are a vice president checking out of the National Naval Medical Center in Bethesda, Maryland, a rescue worker in Siberia, or a crane in a Nebraska cornfield, the equinox touches everyone and everything on the planet at the same time.

It's just that spring doesn't manifest itself at the same

rate. Much depends upon where you physically are on March 20. And if you are driving through central Indiana, and unless you are very attentive, it mostly appears that spring is still a long way off.

"Want to hear more news?" Linda asked, breaking into my thoughts.

"No," I said. "NPR's gone through its morning cycle once already—or are we hearing about Dick Cheney's other leg now?"

"Tunes?" she suggested. "Driver's choice," she reminded me. Dunnes on the Road Rule Number 3. Driver gets to choose the music.

"Bob Seger?" I suggested. It's my default setting.

Linda wrinkled her nose, exercising her passenger prerogative and invoking amendment A to Road Rule Number 3, which is "so long as copilot doesn't strongly object."

We agreed on Cowboy Junkies, and I settled back into my thoughts, contemplating the pastoral landscape as strains of "Miles from Our Home"—nice background music but less thematically apt than the surrounding landscape might suggest—filled the van.

Yes, western Indiana is, geographically speaking, fairly far from southern New Jersey, which Linda and I call home. But the topographically deprived landscape stretching out on all sides of our twenty-one-foot RV (called the Road Pig, or Piggy for short) is no more or less flat than the Coastal Plain of New Jersey, where we live. And the wintered agricultural fields, bordered by woodlands and punctuated at intervals by single-family homes, farm buildings, and microwave relay towers, is much the same landscape that would greet Salem County, New Jersey, commuters en route to offices in Philadelphia, Pennsylvania.

In both places, the landscape is largely dominated by a plant that has struck a balance with the terrestrial creature whose numeric expansion and ability to manipulate the environment have made it one of the most ecologically determining forces on the planet.

The plant, by the way, is corn. It's a highly specialized species of grass and is closely related to the stuff that used to cover most of the prairies of North America. I'll bet you didn't know this.

The terrestrial creature I was referring to is us. I'll bet you did guess that. And since you are one of these creatures, gifted with the deductive (and habitat-manipulating) big brain, I'm also willing to bet that you've already brought that big brain into play, isolated assorted verbal hints and clues scattered throughout this discourse relating to habitat, humans, and ecological forces, and concluded that this book is going to be another one of those environmental diatribes whose theme will be how humans have screwed up royally.

Actually no—or at least that's only a tangential point. In fact, my point right now is somewhat the opposite. We, the terrestrial creature and the corn (and the oak woodlands we allow to stand, and the microwave towers we erect), are not the antitheses of the prairie environment. We, collectively, *are* the prairie environment. Now. In the first decade of the twenty-first century. Three hundred years ago, before the

Conestoga wagon, before the buffalo hunter, before the plow, the landscape was very different—a great sea of grass pocked by islands of trees and cut by broad and seasonally capricious rivers.

That is the romantic image of the prairies we like to nurture. That is what so many of our environmental and habitat restoration initiatives hope to retain or restore. But the great ocean of grass that President Thomas Jefferson purchased from France for about three cents an acre and that conservationists long for is actually of recent geologic origin.

Between ten thousand and eight thousand years ago, much of the land that was prairie back when Lewis and Clark made their exploratory trek was boreal forest—not unlike the great forests that define the northern boundary of the prairies today, or the Black Hills of South Dakota, which are a remnant of that pre-prairie forest. Going back even further, to a point some 20 million years ago, the "prairies" were a savanna, dominated by grasses, dotted with trees, akin to the plains of East Africa today, hosting an array of animals that would not seem out of place in the Serengeti of today: small rhinos, large lions, camels, and the ancestors of modern horses.

Before that, about 45 million years ago, the prairies were host to a warm, moist, tropical forest where proto-monkeys played in the boughs and the blunt-horned, Dumpster-size titanotheres browsed on shrubs. About 50 million years ago, the prairies were undergoing major structural (not just topical) renovation, as a great geologic upheaval in the West (known now as the Rocky Mountains) was rising up and simultaneously wearing down, causing a flood of debris to spill east across the landscape, filling in hollows and generally creating one big, flat, down-sloping plain that remains the foundation of the prairie landscape we know today.

Going back even further, this same midcontinental patch of planet hosted a swampy jungle of ferns and conifers; before that a sand- and salt-blasted desert; and before that and several times over, it was an ocean—the most recent inundation occurring during the Cretaceous Period, between 145 and 65 million years ago, and lasting about eighty thousand years.

People and corn are just the hand that the universe is dealing this corner of the planet, now.

So, relative to the Cretaceous Period, inland seas, and primordial swamps, the landscape bracketing I-74 in western Indiana—now entering eastern Illinois—is not that unlike the landscape that would have greeted Linda and me had we navigated this stretch of planet several hundred years ago. It was then, as it is now, a habitat in transition. The place where the great forests that once blanketed eastern North America begin to founder in a sea of grass.

Where now, instead of big bluestem and other members of the tallgrass prairie community, there is the new dominant tallgrass: corn. And where once there was a landscape dominated by and, in fact, manipulated by bison, now there is us.

Change. It's an integral part of the universe. You can measure it in altering landscapes. You can measure it in the passage of a planet around its sun. You can measure it in . . .

"Rest area," Linda announced, pointing to the friendly, familiar, and welcoming interstate highway sign.

Yep, just like those pioneers moving across the prairies in their Conestoga wagons, cross-country travelers today move between watering holes. Some things don't change.

SPRING IS . . .

When I said that the equinox touches every point of the earth simultaneously, I also said that the season doesn't unfold at the same rate. Where you are in the Northern Hemisphere has a great deal to do with how you find spring and how it finds you.

Close to the equator, spring doesn't mean a whole heck of a lot. At noon, on the first day of spring, the sun is directly overhead, but our planet's star is always high in the sky at this latitude, so the amount of sunlight reaching the earth, and the climate it spawns, varies little throughout the year.

If you are a coffee grower in Colombia, you'll be wearing slacks, long-sleeve shirts, and running shoes no matter what the season.

The farther away from the equator you are, the greater is the seasonal shifting of the sun—from high in the sky to low in the sky; from lots of hours of daylight to markedly fewer, even none! The result is a pronounced seasonality.

If you are a farmer growing corn in Nebraska, you might be sweating in a T-shirt and wearing running shoes in summer; but in winter, you'll be wearing full-length Carhartts and Thinsulate-lined boots (and you'll still be cold!).

The reason for this seasonal shift in sunlight and temperatures has to do with the interrelationship of two things: the angle of the earth and our planet's annual rotation around the sun. Think of the earth as a ball spinning on an axle, or axis. Were the axis straight up and down, and the earth's orbit conducted always on the same plane, the sun's energy would always strike the earth in the same, unvarying manner. It would be strongest directly at the equator (where the light's rays strike the earth's surface directly), diminishing toward the poles.

On such a world, our coffee grower in Colombia would still be wearing slacks and a shirt, but our farmer in Nebraska would be wearing jeans and a jacket and maybe a cap—something suitable for early fall or midspring temperatures, because that is what folks in Nebraska would be experiencing all year long.

Why would the sun's energy be diminishing toward the poles? Because the earth is not a flat plane, it is a globe, a curving plane, so that away from the equator, the surface of the earth curves away from the sun. So while the amount of sunlight reaching the earth is a constant, the surface area that the sun strikes is not. The more the surface of the earth curves away from the sun, the greater surface area there is to be lighted and warmed by the same amount of sunlight, so the less energy there is to go around.

While this is not a perfect analogy, think of sunlight as a pat of butter being spread on a piece of bread from the equator to the poles. At the equator, the butter goes on thick. By the time you get to the poles, it's being scraped thin. In fact, in winter, you run out of butter (sunlight) before you hit the crust (pole).

Okay. That accounts for the unequal distribution of heat and light across the planet. What about seasonality? Remember that the earth is tilted at an angle. In its orbit around the sun, one half of the planet will be inclined toward the sun, so at an angle to receive the lion's share of the sun's energy. The half lying on the other side of the equator angles away from the sun so it receives less energy. One hundred and eighty-two days (or half a year) later, the hemispheric positions are reversed. Now the hemisphere that got shorted before is angled toward the sun, receiving more direct sunlight. It's the other hemisphere that gets skimped.

Another imperfect analogy. Are you familiar with a square-dance step called "do-si-do," in which two partners fold their hands across their chests, lean back on their heels, and circle each other? With their shoulders back and hips projected forward, the dance partners' angle approximates the angle of the earth on its axis.

As the dancers circle each other, for half of the maneuver, it's the shoulders that are inclining toward the partner and the hips that are angled away. For the other half of the revolution, the shoulders are angled away but the hips press closer to the orbiting partner.

Summer is that point when each hemisphere puts its best face forward and gets the lion's share of sunlight. Winter is when it must contend with the solar dregs.

Spring and autumn? These are the equinoxes. The points in the earth year when the sun strikes the equator directly. Sunlight falls in equal measure north and south of the equator.

Sounds reasonable, you think. Except for one thing. If the amounts of energy reaching the earth on the first day of spring and the first day of autumn are equal, how come it's so much colder in the Northern Hemisphere in March than it is in September?

Because, just as it takes time to warm a cold room, it takes time to heat the cold half of a planet, or cool the warm half for that matter. Come March, the Northern Hemisphere is experiencing the effects of several heat-deprived months. The hemisphere, and its surrounding air, are still cold. Sure, most of the north has received sunlight over the winter months, but, relative to the amount of sunlight reaching the equatorial regions and the Southern Hemisphere, not much; and in years when extensive portions of Northern Hemisphere are subjected to a standing snowpack, much of the sun's energy is reflected back into space. It doesn't warm the earth; the warmth is not transferred to the surrounding air.

In short, there is a lag time. March, across much of North America, is the odd month out, the rough, transitional month in between winter and spring. Coming in like a lion, and sometimes going out that way, too.

Whoever said that March goes out like a lamb must have lived someplace other than the North American prairies.

It was Linda's turn to drive now. My turn to shift my attention away from the road and focus on the landscape unfolding at close to sixty-five miles per hour. The woodlands, a mix of oaks, hickories, and a smattering of other eastern deciduous trees, were gray and bare.

But now, as we traveled through Illinois, even the remnants of the great eastern deciduous forests seemed to be diminishing with every mile. More and more the landscape was becoming dominated by agricultural fields. Trees were relegated to the border, defining fields the color and rough texture of stretched burlap, except for those that had already been disked or plowed in preparation for this year's seed.

Some grasses, including most native prairie grasses, are perennial. Spring's touch brings their dormant essence back to life. Others, including many nonnative species and corn, which is not an invasive but a highly modified native species, are called "annuals." They spring from seeds that must be dispersed or sown every year.

But on this last day of winter, and first day of spring, most of the great grain fields that were once native grasslands stood as winter and the harvesting machines had left them. Withered and brown. Light brown or dark. This is how most highway travelers see them, just . . .

Brown. Tired old brown. Boring old brown.

Why is this? What is it about this color that elicits such disdain—makes businessmen buying suits look to any color but; makes neighbors seeing the color being applied to the house across the street see real estate values falling?

When Detroit rolls out its new models, does anyone ever put a brown car on the showroom floor? Does any car manufacturer, except Rolls-Royce, even offer a car in brown?

And after newly infatuated young couples have worked out core matters relating to favorite music groups, best cell phone service, favorite ice cream, the existence of God, and they finally get around to the question "What's your favorite color?" has there ever been a time when brown has trumped red, or blue, or even green?

So what *is* the root of our antipathy for brown?

Does it harken back to those early years when dirt and mud pies were just about the best things in the whole universe but your admonishing mom turned the tables and made dirt dirty (your first four-letter word)?

Or does it have its root in what is for many their first experiment in chemistry? When in art class, at a time the teacher wasn't looking, you mixed all the colors in the poster paint jars anticipating spectral glory but all you got was something that looked like mud.

As we drove through Illinois, then Iowa, and on into Nebraska, brown was the color of the world on the last day of winter. Measured in hours or miles, it's a lot of sameness, and I can see why it is that people who are weary of winter and eager for spring are also eager to see this color of anticipation pass—because that is what brown is.

The color of the waiting earth.

Many years ago, sometime after my first failed chemistry experiment but before fumbling discussions relating to favorite ice cream flavors and recently professed beliefs in agnosticism became really, really important, I read a story in our grammar school reader about a young girl who was going to a prairie school dance but had, as poor fortune had it, nothing to wear but a homemade dress that was plain old homespun brown.

Of course she was mortified.

A friend became aware of her classmate's misfortune and came to the rescue. The dress the friend was wearing to the dance was a spiffy, seasonally calibrated yellow. As fortune had it, after the dress was cut and sewn, there was material left over. "I'll bet," said the unhappy girl's friend, "that a yellow trim on the sash of that brown dress would look real sweet."

Okay, maybe she didn't say *sweet*. But the sentiment was similar and the results the same. The yellow trim, set against that plain brown backdrop, was fetching indeed, and the wearer had a great time at the party.

What was the lesson of the story (because all the stuff in those reading books was supposed to instill values, or teach valuable coping lessons, so that we could all grow up to be well-adjusted and productive members of society)? Put faith in friends? If you have lemons, make lemonade? I don't know. I just remember it as a pretty dumb story, and, besides, it was mostly about girls.

One thing I did learn is that the way to make a color really stand out is to set it against a backdrop of plain old brown.

And on this last day of winter that was also the first day

of spring, the colors signaling transition were already at hand, for those who knew how to read the landscape. On the tattered cattails bordering roadside marshes, red-winged blackbirds were unfurling ember-colored epaulets, flying the red banner of spring. On half a hundred sun-warmed hillsides, red-tailed hawks were catching thermals, riding spring aloft. And on roadside wires, half-yellow, half-brown meadowlarks were throwing their whistled taunt into the sky, adding the weight of their voices in favor of the season that was still, officially, several hours away.

If you looked very closely beneath the veil of brown running out on both sides of the highway, you could catch, on wooded hillsides, the first faint blush of color emanating from swelling buds. And in the fields, beneath their veil there was green new growth poking up amid the old. Spring on this twentieth of March was not just in the air. It was embedded in the earth. It was all around us.

Incidentally, just as predicted and after about thirteen hours of driving, spring 2007 officially arrived on the prairies of central Nebraska at 7:07 P.M. CDT. By that time, the fields were going from brown to shadow gray.

No. It had nothing to do with the lateness of the day. But it did have a great deal to do with the changing of the season.

Chapter 2
Kearney, Nebraska

The Crucible of Cranes

Westbound commuter traffic out of Grand Island, Nebraska, was waning in measure with the afternoon sunlight. It was setting up to be a beautiful sunset, but after thirteen hours of driving, all we had eyes for was the Nebraska Game and Parks campground still an hour away.

Well, almost all we had eyes for.

"Look at all the cranes," Linda announced in tones that would not seem out of place if she were announcing the Second Coming.

"Wow" was the first thing that came to mind and, not coincidentally, the first word out of my mouth.

Standing about two hundred yards off I-80, their shadow-colored forms hardly visible amid the stubble, were a couple of hundred feeding cranes. Eyes calibrated, we quickly realized that beyond the first bunch there were other cranes. And in the air, at several levels, more—perhaps five hundred birds in all.

A small down payment on the estimated five to six hundred thousand lesser sandhill cranes that pack into the Platte River for several weeks of carbohydrate loading preparatory to making their migratory passage to Arctic and subarctic breeding grounds. It is the largest such concentration of cranes in the world, and it draws, annually, thousands of visitors who travel to the Grain Belt communities of Grand Island and Kearney to witness the spectacle.

"More cranes to the south," Linda announced. "Lots."

And there were. On the ground, but especially in the air. It was getting late, quitting time for cranes. After a busy day of knocking back kernels of corn, the birds were beating wings toward the Platte. There, in a two-hour frenzy of motion and sound, they would crowd the sandy bars and shank-deep shallows in one of the planet's most celebrated aggregations of living things and one of North America's most ridiculed rivers.

Half water, half sand; "too wet to plow and too thick to drink" is how one Platte detractor once described it. But my all-time favorite reference to this prairie river stems from its analogous comparison to one of Nebraska's favorite sons—newspaper editor and three-time presidential candidate William Jennings Bryan, touted by many as the finest orator of his day, most celebrated for his famous "Cross of Gold" speech, in which he argued forcefully (and unsuccessfully) against a U.S. currency based solely on the gold standard. A Bryan detractor is said to have ascribed to him the properties of the Platte: "an inch deep and a mile wide at the mouth."

I actually have a family link to the famous Nebraskan newspaperman (and so, by association, the river). When she was an eminently catchable young lady, my grandmother Dunne, then Rose Powers, attended finishing school outside Washington, D.C.—a practice befitting the daughter of the man who owned several Chicago theaters. Part of the curriculum involved dinner at the White House, and there, as fortune had it and the story goes, young Miss Powers sat next to a young William Jennings Bryan.

Said my grandmother of the occasion and of Mr. Bryan (and never without a smirk on her face), "He was the most boring man I ever met."

This from a woman who married a patent attorney. Back to the Platte.

"Let's do a running count," I said to Linda. "You keep an eye to the right."

By the time we reached the turnoff to Rowe Sanctuary at Gibbon, Nebraska, the total had topped ten thousand birds, which sounds like a lot and is a lot.

But if the volume of staging cranes along the Platte were converted to linear feet and if ten thousand birds was rated "an inch deep," then our ten-thousand-bird ante would leave us 59,999 inches, or approximately five thousand feet, short of a full migratory population.

Just about the width of the Platte at its mouth.

Why here? Why now? What is it about this stretch of prairie river, running between Kearney and Grand Island, that is so attractive to cranes? Great natural spectacles don't just happen. There is rhyme. There is reason. There are, for cranes as for all living things, needs that must be met and situations and circumstances that meet them.

Let's work backward. Let's use the "big brain," and as a deductive footing the premise that an ongoing, annual assemblage of half a million–plus birds (which just happen to have survived on this planet for longer than our species) is not a fluke.

In the broadest sense, the cranes are here because the habitat is right for them. Cranes are open-country birds. You would not expect half a million cranes to be staging in an eastern deciduous forest. You would expect them on open prairie.

Also significant. Nebraska is right on the route linking crane wintering and breeding areas. It is convenient, a way station, reducing the rigors all voyagers who are obliged to travel great distances must endure. Have you ever wondered why the celebrated tourist trap known as South of the Border is located about halfway between the population centers of the Northeast and the vacation mecca that is Florida—a two-day drive? Think about it.

Also important. The opportunities presented by the Platte and its environment are stable and predictable. Sure, the lands of midcontinental North America have experienced extensive changes over time (and few have been so rapid and dramatic as those that have transpired in the last 150 years). But now, for a number of reasons, the Platte offers migrating cranes a stable, crane-supportive environment. Many of those reasons are explained in the exhibit room at the Audubon Center at Rowe Sanctuary, located on the banks of the Platte, about five miles south of Gibbon, Nebraska.

The center, built with environmentally friendly strawbale construction and open year-round, sees twelve to fifteen thousand visitors annually, most in a four-week period known to the staff as "Crane Season." In this regard, it is much like several other very celebrated interpretive centers whose primary focus is a relatively brief and natural phenomenon. But unlike, say, Hawk Mountain, Pennsylvania, a two-hour drive from New York or Philadelphia, Gibbon, Nebraska, is slightly more out of the way for most of the planet's human inhabitants. While a number of local residents and many local school groups annually visit the center, most people who visit Rowe do so as an act of volition—sometimes extreme volition.

A map in the center is dotted by multicolored pushpins, stuck in Paraguay, Kenya, Iraq, Russia, China, Japan, Australia, New Zealand, and many if not most of the nation-states constituting the European Community.

The pins are retired every year. The countries just recounted constitute the origins of visitors during the first half of Crane Season 2007. Each one represents a visitor or visitors who traveled here expressly to see cranes.

They aren't here for the corn.

Then again, maybe they are! The March and early April concentration of cranes in the Cornhusker State is not a coincidence.

Kent Skaggs, office manager at Rowe, is just shy of middle age, crops his hair short, and sports a trim beard and mustache that might be called professorial on a less athletic and outdoorsy person. Don't let the title "office manager" fool you. Kent, a native Nebraskan (a label not uncommon in these parts), has a degree in biology and an employment history that includes earlier stints with the National Audubon Society and Nebraska Game and Parks. He has also served as the "Crane Host" for the Kearney Chamber of Commerce at Fort Kearny State Historical Park during the period of the annual crane migration, the biological centerpiece for the Spring Rivers & Wildlife Celebration (AKA the Crane Festival).

This celebration, ongoing since 1970, is arguably North America's oldest bird festival, second only, perhaps, to the New Jersey Audubon Society's Cape May Autumn Weekend, which was first celebrated in 1946.

In November 2000, Kent returned to the staff at Rowe, where he is joined by Assistant Manager Bill Taddicken, Education Director Keanna Leonard, and the newly appointed director, Brad Mellema.

Why am I telling you all this? To impress upon you the significance of having someone like Kent offer me half an hour of his time at the time of the year when he and a skeletal staff are working ten- and twelve-hour days, seven days a week, riding herd on fifteen thousand visitors.

And now you begin to understand why facilities such as Rowe prize their buffering cadre of volunteers, of which Rowe boasts many.

"Let's go down the hall, where we'll be less disturbed," said Kent, directing us away from the nature store, which was doing a brisk business selling anything and everything that even hinted of cranes.

I'm a professional; Kent's a professional. I knew he'd level with me, but I was surprised not only by his candor but also by the image-shattering truths in his disclosures. The cranes, the great natural phenomenon that people travel thousands of miles to witness, are also far from being natural, if by natural you mean pristine and unsullied by the hand of man.

First, as Kent allowed, the birds are unnaturally concentrated. Once, before nine major dams were built across the Platte, roosting habitat was more generous and the birds more dispersed. Cranes roost in shallow water, a defense against predators, and they are particular about water depth. The Big Bend stretch between Kearney and Grand Island (a distance of approximately fifty land, not nautical, miles) offers birds the best wet footing now—providing spring rains are moderately generous and the people controlling the water flow from the dams are, too. In pre-dam times, the river was a mile wide, and, at times, in parts of the floodplain, the marshy and ponded corridor stretched ten, even fifteen miles across. Now a quarter-mile-wide strand accommodates most of the river's flow through the Big Bend corridor.

Also, cranes are picky about their landscaping. Just as migrating cranes aren't partial to forest, they have, by natural extension, an aversion to narrow, tree- and brush-crowded riverbanks. On the pre-dam Platte, large bank-flanking cottonwood trees were mostly absent, present primarily on larger islands. Periodic large-scale spring floods scoured the river's banks, leaving in their wake open, crane-friendly vistas. In this age of competing water interests and restricted river flow, trees have the latitude to root and grow, with the result that, in order to offer suitable roosting habitat for cranes, the riverside trees and brush must be cut and removed.

What the river used to do for nothing, now heavy machinery does at a cost. Recently, a six-hundred-million-dollar pot of federal money was allocated for much-needed river enhancement and restoration, to be divided between the states of Colorado and Nebraska. And yes, certainly an alternative to this expense might be simply to remove the dams and restore the Platte to its natural, capricious, tree-trimming flow.

But that would be a very hard sell to the many farmers who use Platte River water to irrigate flanking cornfields, whose annual yield is measured in hundreds of millions of bushels and whose net income supports families who have lived along the Platte for several generations. It would be especially difficult to persuade farmers to reduce their water use and limit their corn yields at a time when prices are at a ten-year high, spurred in no small part by the growing demand for ethanol.

Let's also not forget the loss to a worldwide consumer base that uses corn and corn-based products as additives or ingredients in almost everything these days—from soft drinks and TV dinners to soups, hot dogs, salad dressings, mayonnaise, margarine, and, of course, the ethanol-enhanced gasoline that is promoted as a way of reducing our nation's dependence upon Gulf oil.

You would probably also have a tough time selling the idea to the cranes, because this is precisely the point where the line between natural and unnatural is drawn very fine. The truth is that the great masses of cranes are concentrated here precisely because of the bounty of corn. Mechanical harvesting is an effective but profligate operation. A portion of every year's crop goes back to the land as unharvested waste, and this libation to nature not only is enough to support a healthy population of migrating geese but also fuels the migration of cranes.

It is estimated that between 80 and 90 percent of the food ingested by cranes along the Platte is the same stuff you probably put in your cereal bowl this morning. The birds stay two to four weeks. Forage all day, roost at night. During this time they increase their body weight by about 18 percent. This is the fuel they will burn en route to the breeding grounds. The balance of the birds' nutritional intake is provided by insects, snails, worms, and any other small finned, furred, or scaled critters that find their way to within the stabbing reach of a crane's spikelike bill.

But in the balance, happy about the broader implications or not, the migration of North America's midcontinent population of sandhill cranes runs on corn. While the populations of most of the birds and animals that once thrived on the prairies have suffered as a result of the habitat changes visited upon the biome by our species, the sandhill crane, a veteran survivalist with at least 2.5 million years notched on its shanks, is happy to award *Homo sapiens* nine pinions up.

Why not a perfect ten? Well, in a perfect world, cranes would probably like to see fewer high-tension lines (which seine them out of the air), and maybe the species' removal from the ranks of migratory game birds, and, perhaps more Texas cotton fields converted to sorghum.

But from a population standpoint, these are minor points. Sandhill crane numbers are, at least, stable and probably increasing.

For now. In this age of this world. On the new prairie.

For Kent, his fellow Audubon staff members, and the host of crane volunteers, this age, of this world, held about two more weeks of crunch time and perhaps five thousand hopeful and expectant visitors to go. Why do they do it? Why does he?

"To offer people a fantastic wildlife experience."

And a natural one, too! As natural as the American prairies today.

FOR THE LOVE OF CRANES

So what is it about cranes in general, and sandhill cranes in particular, that inspires such ardor and admiration, not only among bird watchers but from people of all walks of life?

Part of the appeal has to do with size. Cranes are large birds, standing over three feet high. They are easily noticed and easily observed. For some reason, our species lavishes more attention on megafauna than on smaller animals; bison and turkeys turn heads; ground squirrels and chestnut-collared longspurs commonly do not.

Also, cranes are birds of open habitats, making them fairly conspicuous, and in winter and in migration they are flocking birds. Great aggregations of living things attract us and inspire us. The greater the number, the better.

Here is the curious thing. Overlook its size, take away its supporting numbers, and there is little overtly magnificent about a solitary sandhill crane. Shaped like a long-necked vase and posed on stiltlike legs, the bird resembles a heron or an egret.

But a stocky heron. The neck is long but not sinuous, the legs long but not lanky. Head turned down, the bird looks and moves like a hump-backed camel; and standing erect, it moves with a bumpkinish, loose-jointed ease, not the slow, theatrical strides of one of the aquatic wading birds.

And the color! Mostly gray. An eye-defeating gray, touched with traces of ocher and rust, rendering the birds almost invisible even when they're standing in an open cornfield. I have often thought that if one of the camo companies wanted to develop a pattern ideally suited for open country, all they would have to do is replicate the plumage of this shadow-colored bird.

Small, brightly colored birds, like cardinals and breeding-plumage goldfinches, are more likely to catch our eye and win our favor than gray ones, even big gray ones. So what else is it about this bird that makes thousands of people cross continents, even oceans, just to see it?

I'm only guessing here, but I believe part of the crane's appeal is anthropomorphic. I think we see in cranes—or project onto them—a lot of admirable traits, traits that remind us of ourselves and make us feel close to them. Cranes are monogamous, and they mate for life, social qualities that are still admired and aspired to in our society (climbing divorce rates and the denial of presidential candidates notwithstanding).

Also, cranes have tight-knit family units, with young birds traveling with parents for nine or ten months after hatching. Search the world over, and you'll find that family scores high on the scale of human values—whether the accent falls on immediate or extended family groups. There is loyalty in cranes, and we admire it.

Furthermore, many of the world's cranes, including lesser sandhills, are great voyagers, great risk takers—and from Christopher Columbus to Warren Buffett to *Who Wants to Be a Millionaire* America does love risk takers. The annual migrations of these birds, from the Arctic and subarctic regions of Canada, Alaska, and western Siberia to wintering areas in Texas, New Mexico, and northern Mexico, cover thousands of miles, with those birds breeding in western Siberia traversing no fewer than thirty-five hundred peril-fraught miles.

All these things endear cranes to us. And to all these compelling attributes add one more: the birds are fairly tame. While not frightless—in fact in many parts of their breeding and wintering range the birds are hunted—cranes are habituated enough to people and their activity patterns to allow us to approach close enough to view them with or without the aid of optics.

We like to be trusted by wild things. Their trust supports our view that we are the generous, noble, trustworthy custodians of the earth we believe ourselves to be.

But all these qualities together still cannot account for the partiality, the almost visceral bond, our species projects upon these birds. There is still one quality missing. The catalytic link that joins us soul to soul. That is sound. There are very few sounds that are as stirring or evocative as the call of the sandhill crane.

Make that *calls*. The vocal array of sandhill cranes is fairly extensive, generally broken down into three subcategories: trills and purrs, loud rattles, and nonrattle calls.

I spent one evening isolating and transcribing the sounds of cranes coming to roost. It's not the best way, and surely not the right way, to experience the spectacle (you might as well try to dissect a miracle), but I was amazed at the array and then surprised, after having spent hundreds of hours within earshot of cranes, that I could still be surprised by calls I never attributed to the birds.

There was, of course, the classic croaking purr or gargled trill that always reminds me of the creak of a wooden hinged gate. There was the high, somewhat breathy trill of young birds (reminiscent of the food-begging cries of many other bird species, ranging from gulls to penguins). And then there were the odd cries. A trumpeting bray that recalled great blue heron. A two-noted honk that I had to confirm was not being made by a Canada goose. A hoarse, gull-like keening, a limpkinlike wail, a two-noted bleat, and a short, hollow-sounding series of percussive taps.

But this academic exercise was just that. Breaking down the vocal components of the sound of ten or twenty or fifty thousand sandhill cranes all assembled in one place, at one time, makes about as much sense as isolating the colors of the spectrum when what you are seeking, in your heart of hearts, is blinding white light.

What people love most about cranes is not the variety of sounds per se. It is the harmonic din that is felt as much as heard, that envelopes and penetrates you and plays you like a harp, because it strums chords in us that lie very deep.

The source of this vocal array is the crane's trachea. Unusually long, looped like a French horn, and tucked behind the sternum, it allows the bird a range of amplification and pitches.

I have seen people cry at the mercy of this sound. I have cried myself.

I am a pretty fair wordsmith. With a little thought and flourish, I can usually come up with words that can convey an experience or at least suggest one to the mind of a reader. Here I've met my match.

The conjoined sound of sandhill cranes is a wild sound whose reception only starts in the brain, then penetrates deep into the blood. It might be that it stirs something in us that harkens back to the days when our ancestors roamed the East African plains.

There were cranes then, too. In Kenya, one of the earliest sounds of the approaching dawn and the end of night is the cry of the crowned crane. If you hear this sound, it means one very important thing: you survived the night.

It is not a gabble. It is not fanfare. It is not something you can compare to or relate to if you have not heard it. But here, on the banks of the Platte, you can hear it every March.

The creaking and croaking of half a million northbound cranes—a sound akin to a giant door opening upon one season and closing on another.

STRAW-BALE BLIND, TAKEN SOUL

"We're going into crane country," Beezy, our crane interpreter and sanctuary volunteer volunteered. "We'll want to be just as quiet as we can be."

None of the twenty-odd visitors assembled in the parking area contradicted her. All of us had our sights set on witnessing the spectacle of birds coming to roost, and nobody wanted to be responsible for screwing it up—however slight the chances. The professionals at Rowe, meaning the staff and seasonal interpretive volunteers, offer thousands of visitors unsurpassed intimacy with cranes during the four weeks that constitute crane season. Clearly, they have developed a system for viewing the birds that works. In no small part, it is the product of the procedural pains taken to ensure that our human presence will not intrude upon the birds.

This is just another way of saying "won't scare them away," but the ethic of minimal impact is genuine and part of the natural history interpretation culture worldwide. As the name *sanctuary* implies, the Iain Nicolson Audubon Center (also known as Rowe Sanctuary) regards cranes as its primary constituents. People, even dues-paying members and income-generating visitors, come second.

If you had any doubts, all you had to do was look at the tall, level-eyed (but otherwise very friendly) volunteer named Beezy.

"I want to get out to the blinds before the birds begin to arrive," she announced. And we did. Walking the several-hundred-yard mowed walkway that cut a path through the winter-withered grass, we entered the ten-by-fifty-foot straw-bale blind with nary a word spoken, scuffed foot, cough, or sneeze.

The straw-covered floor muffled the footsteps of all who hurried to secure a place at the viewing slits (and it was all). Our group included about a dozen English majors from the University of Nebraska, who were completing a writing assignment for their required course on nature writing. Everyone had a notepad; only three had binoculars.

Rounding out our ranks were several couples ranging in

age from thirty to I-wouldn't-dare-presume, several women who were in some fashion acquainted, and another woman, who seemed by herself. The license plates on the cars in the lot revealed that some visitors had come from Colorado, Wyoming, Minnesota, Wisconsin, Mississippi, Iowa, and Alberta (although some of these drivers and passengers were scattered among other viewing blinds). Most of the nonstudent viewers in our blind did have binoculars. One had a spotting scope.

Their optics would come in handy, at least initially. The river in front of us was about two hundred yards wide, with a deeper channel midway across and a network of sandbars and braided channels. To the east and west, the river stretched about two miles in either direction—about as far as the unaided eye can see. The birds roosting on this stretch of river commonly begin to land well downstream and finish their nightly arrival by putting in directly in front of the blind.

But it has to be a good night. And you have to be pretty lucky.

As we jockeyed for position, paying only slight attention to the croaking calls emanating from the small flocks of cranes flying past, Beezy began her litany—a discourse offering a cursory overview of the natural history of *Grus canadensis*, the sandhill crane.

I didn't really listen; I was probably the only person in the blind who didn't. I already know a fair amount about sandhill cranes and cranes in general, know that cranes rank among the oldest of living birds, with fossil records going back 35 to 40 million years. Remains of birds in the genus *Grus*, in which both sandhill and the rare and endangered whooping crane are classed, have been dated back to better than 9 million years ago.

Our species, *Homo sapiens*, by comparison, has been around for about 200,000 to 250,000 years, and members of our genus for perhaps 2.4 million years.

I've studied sandhills in their favored wintering areas on the playa wetlands of Texas on their breeding territories in Alaska. In the spring of 1982, while conducting a migratory hawk census on the coast of Alaska, I got to witness the spectacle of tens of thousands of migrating sandhills as they threaded a path between the Malaspina Glacier and the Pacific Ocean, en route to breeding areas in the Yukon-Kuskoquim Delta region of Alaska and, presumably, other northern and western regions, including Siberia.

Those Alaskan migrants were part of the same population of lesser sandhill cranes that stage on the Platte.

Yes, I knew these things and other facets of crane biology, but the reason I was here, and the reason you are reading this, now, has nothing to do with facts or knowledge. It has to do with wonder. It has to do with wow!

It so happens that this was not my first experience in a crane-viewing blind on the banks of the Platte River. Twelve years ago, Linda and I were marshaled into just such a setting, and we stood in the growing twilight as thousands of birds dropped in before us in a throat-tightening, eye-welling, soul-taking avalanche of descending forms and rising sound.

I am no stranger to great spectacles of nature. I've traveled far; I've seen much. Caribou migrations in the Arctic; half a million migrating hawks in a single September day in Corpus Christi, Texas; a blizzard of monarch butterflies going by at the rate of five hundred a minute at Cape May, New Jersey; king penguins whose numbers filled and overflowed the Salisbury Plain on the island of South Georgia; a million and a half short-tailed shearwaters feeding amid forty bubble-feeding humpback whales in the cold waters of the northern Pacific.

But I have never been so transfixed and so emotionally undone as I was that night in a blind beside the Platte. I was here hoping that there is enough magic in the world to be so captivated again.

Shortly after 7:00 P.M., the first roosting birds began to appear, upriver, little more than a mile away. They arrived in small flocks and pairs, parachuting in on set wings.

The students, clustered at the far end of the blind and busily describing their existential experiences, seemed unaware. The older viewers, better positioned, were more attentive but not enchanted.

There is a threshold to human awareness. A natural experience has be x close or y impressive to crack our twenty-first-century veneer. What happened at 7:15 placed us at the intersection of both axes.

The volume of calls suddenly increased, and what had been a medley of croaking voices became an amorphous roar. I looked upriver to see a mass of birds arriving and descending, vaulting the birds already on the river, landing in ever-encroaching ranks.

"Do you have any idea how many there are?" a voice whispered. I did a quick estimate, counting in blocks of a thousand.

"About ten, maybe twelve thousand," I gauged. So large a number, so early in the evening, surprised even Beezy.

"This is really good," she confided. "The best in this blind this season."

"Wowwww," the whisperer breathed but this time didn't whisper. While it hardly mattered (the volume of sound emanating from the birds ensured that), his exclamation did make me realize that his had been the only audible expression in the blind. Everyone else was too captivated to speak, and the number of pens and pencils poised motionless over the pads in the hands of students attested to the fact that the experience was too arresting to allow them to write.

Even with a grade at stake!

Binoculars hung suspended from necks. Couples reached for their partners' hands. The woman who seemed by herself was poised at the very north end of the blind, mouth open and eyes, for as long as I watched, unblinking.

A taken soul.

The sun was lower now, the birds closer, almost across from us. Almost too many birds to fit on the bank. New arrivals were being edged into the river, the color of which, in the deepening evening, was changing from silver to salmon while the banks were shifting from sand to shadow gray.

I glanced down our human ranks again. Looking at faces, looking at expressions, looking at people too moved to write or express. I glanced back out of the viewing slit again and saw that the birds had now filled the opposing bank and were flanking us on the left.

I checked my watch. Noted the time on the pad. Considered going over to be closer to the woman who stood in the corner, to see if she'd blinked yet. And then . . .

The entire river lifted from its banks in an eruption of wings and an ascending avalanche of forms and sound. The earth seeking communion with the sky.

That's when it happened, I guess. Or didn't happen, if you prefer. That's when I stopped wondering about the people in the blind, writing about the people in the blind, even being aware that there *were* other people in the blind.

That is when all existence was drawn down to two points and a single braided line woven of motion, mass, and sound. Then the line became short. Then it became gone. And then, just as it happened twelve years ago, I was taken.

The last notation on my pad reads 7:45. The rest of the page is blank. I learned this only sometime later, after realizing that Beezy was asking me a question, asking whether, in my estimate, it was all right to leave the blind yet.

"With the birds so close?"

"Yes," I heard myself say, and with this utterance I returned to the world as I'd left it, with the host of shadow-colored birds upon one side, the far side, and I, again, on the other. But the woman standing in the far corner was unmoving, her mouth still drawn in a silent O, still taken.

I would have given anything to be her.

At Beezy's bidding, we collected our things and departed, single-file, leaving the blind, the river, and the birds. She, the woman in the corner, came last of all.

And now, hours later, as I struggle to find words that are usually so easy to find, I find myself wondering . . .

How did the students do with their essays? How does the woman in the corner fare this morning, and what side of the river is she on?

But most of all I am wondering how a writer goes about retrieving and then recounting the soul-searing wonders never transcribed on a page marked only "7:45."

How does a writer go about interviewing a taken soul?

CHAPTER 3

Pawnee Buttes, Colorado

WINTER STRIKES BACK

It was rainy and a bit nasty when we left Kearney, Nebraska, warm and sunny by the time we reached Crow Valley Campground in the Pawnee National Grassland of Colorado. The bud-swollen branches of the campground's cottonwoods scratched at a clear blue sky. The flanking prairie showed just a touch of green beneath its shroud of wintered grass.

We were en route to the town of Lamar in southeastern Colorado but decided to take a hundred-mile detour because the weather was so great and the forecast for southeastern Colorado sounded not so great.

NOAA Weather Radio was promising strong thunderstorms, lightning, and hail, and had issued a tornado watch for the Lamar region. All the ingredients for a bad time in a small RV adrift in the middle of the prairies. The prediction for the northeastern part of the state was less daunting. Temperatures falling into the low thirties by dawn. Slight chance of rain or snow showers after midnight. Nothing we and our spunky Road Pig haven't weathered before.

We arrived at Crow Valley to find three other parties of campers already entrenched and our favorite spot taken. A surprise! In late March, in midweek, we'd been sure we'd find one of our favorite places in the cosmos empty. But we'd forgotten that many Colorado school districts were on their spring break, and the weather in the state over much of March had been unseasonably mild.

"Haven't seen a day below freezing in over a month," one Colorado resident bragged to us (and he wasn't lying by much). By all the signs—clear skies, warm temperatures, American robins singing up a ... uh ... forget that one—the streak seemed destined to last until October.

"Let's head on up to Pawnee Buttes," I suggested.

"Let's," Linda agreed. Why settle for a valley when you can have the heights? And on national grasslands, camping is not restricted to established campgrounds. And the view! Looking east off the escarpment as far as the physical limits of a curving planet provide. It makes the backdrop to Robert Redford and Meryl Streep's picnic scene in the movie *Out of Africa* look like a stage prop. (And yes. I've been there. "On location" as they say. The Buttes beat the Mara hands down.)

So we left the shelter of Crow Valley and headed for the Buttes.

Is there anyone reading this who hasn't figured out

where this story is heading yet? Then you are as dumb as Linda and I. Dumb enough to stand right in the path of Old Man Winter's fist when he stages a classic end-of-the-season comeback known far and wide as the Late Winter Storm.

WHERE SEASONS COLLIDE

Spring is grist for the poet's mill, a playground for young love, a time of renewal, rebirth, and . . .

Spring is a battlefield where two eternally polarized seasons, winter and summer, both wielding great and opposing air masses, battle for supremacy. The prairies are where these opposing forces clash, and in no place is the epic contest more violent and dramatic than on the Great Plains of North America.

To understand the war, you must understand the underlying conflict, which begins, as most conflicts do, with an unequal apportionment of resources. As it relates to seasons and weather, that resource is the most important commodity on Earth—the solar energy that puts the oomph in our atmosphere and supports life on Earth.

In winter, when the Northern Hemisphere is deprived of solar energy, large landmasses, such as North America and Europe-Asia, cool more rapidly than the adjacent oceans. The result is the formation of different pressure centers, with large, cold, dry, and stable air masses (high-pressure centers) forming over the landmasses and low-pressure centers forming over the adjacent waters around the Aleutians and Iceland.

If you've listened to weather reports, you have undoubtedly heard meteorologists refer to the "Canadian high," usually in reference to an ensuing period of cold weather as the cold, sometimes Arctic cold, air associated with the winter pattern bulges south in the form of a cold front. These fronts sometimes, but rarely, penetrate as far south as the Yucatán Peninsula; wherever they travel, they blanket the region with cold, dry, stable air.

It might not be pleasant, but it is the classic weather pattern of winter.

In spring, the tables are turned. Steadily increasing sunlight reaching the Northern Hemisphere causes the ocean waters of the Pacific, the Atlantic, and (of particular significance to the prairie weather) the Gulf of Mexico to heat up and the geopolitical ambitions of the subtropical air masses riding above them to look north. At intervals, warm, moist air from the Gulf of Mexico and the tropics surges north across the lands east of the Rocky Mountains as warm fronts, treating the landscape to bursts of spring as the summer pattern develops.

When this pattern really takes hold, in June, July, and August, the hot, sultry weather of the summer pattern isn't very pleasant, either, but we tend to overlook this in the spring.

Arctic and subtropical air masses are not the only forces at play across the prairies. In spring and summer, dry desert winds emanating from the southwest sometimes enter and complicate the meteorological fray, and later in the season, by early to mid-July, tropical moisture welling up out of Mexico brings to southwestern areas monsoon rains that sometimes affect the prairies.

But in spring, the season breaker and weather maker is the protracted tug-of-war between the forces of the entrenched cold air laying claim to the north and the warm, insurgent air invading from the south. Spring is the protracted period of conflict—the war between winter and summer, if you will. Weather is the day-to-day courses of the battle—sometimes waged in tumultuous clashes, sometimes in minor skirmishes. It changes with the tide of battle, changes like the weather, and what you experience on any given day depends upon the course of the war and where you are.

If you are in occupied territory, the weather will be stable and cold (if you are where the winter pattern dominates) or warm (if the forces of spring have overrun and secured your region). On the other hand, if it is your ill fortune to be on the front lines, where cold, dry air from the north collides with warm, moist air from the south, you have a front-row seat to one of the planet's epic dramas.

On March 28, Pawnee Buttes wasn't just front-row seats. It was somewhere between the orchestra pit and center stage.

STUPID IS AS STUPID DOES, OR

BOYWHATAFANTASTICVIEW

It was a balmy sixty-four degrees when we reached the lower parking area for Pawnee Buttes—as far as we could travel ethically and physically. The need to offer several species of cliff-nesting raptors privacy constituted the ethical constraint. The locked gate, prompting compliance on the part of less ethical or illiterate visitors, was there for reinforcement.

When Linda and I had first come here, in the late eighties, there was no gate, and there were no restrictions and no limits to the level of stress levied upon nesting prairie falcons, golden eagles, American kestrels, great horned owls, and other species by viewers and rock climbers. Now, from March 1 until June 30, access to the escarpment is denied. It's not much of a hardship. The view from the lower lot is pretty fine, and the two-mile hiking trail leading out to the buttes is well maintained and well marked (not that anyone is likely to get lost).

"How about here?" Linda suggested, gesturing toward a slightly sloping outcropping already scarred by tire tracks.

"The view is great," I agreed, "but the pitch is, too. If we park there, we'll need to get out levelers. Over there looks flatter."

Linda smiled, widely enough for me to ask why.

"Because that's where I wanted to go, but I knew if I said it you'd want to go someplace else."

Of course I denied it was true.

"Over there" was flatter, and while it was no less sheltered, what angle there was led down (not up) to the packed dirt road. If conditions turned gnarly, and the substrate slippery, at least we'd have gravity on our side.

We parked. Got settled. Got out a bottle of wine to help

us enjoy the view, the approaching evening, and storm clouds gathering to the south and east. The winds were getting stronger, blowing twenty to twenty-five miles per hour from the south. But the van made a good barrier, and except for occasional eddies, we were well protected from dust, grit, and windblown pieces of grass that like to sully a not-so-bad California Cabernet.

"That's a good one," I said, gesturing with a glass toward one world-class thunderhead that was probably making a shambles of all the wash hung on all the clotheslines in western Nebraska.

"Been watching it," she said. "Lightning to the south and *look!*"

An adult golden eagle popped into view, flying low and slow into the winds rising up along the rim of the escarpment—a hunting technique that combines stealth and surprise, and one whose effectiveness many a jackrabbit or bighorn lamb has appreciated only after the fact. Sometimes golden eagles hunt in pairs. This one was solitary, and its modest size and present circumstances suggested it was the male of the local pair. Now, in late March, the female would almost certainly be incubating eggs on the escarpment.

We watched the eagle for several minutes. Sipping our wine. Listening to the sound of a western meadowlark over the wind. Watching the distant cloud show and not being particularly concerned. After all, the storms were very distant. The edge of the front was well to the east. And weather systems track east, not west. Right?

The winds, still blowing strong from the south, should have served as a warning. The long, high, and increasingly impressive band of clouds growing in size and darkening in color just behind us didn't go unnoticed.

"Looks like you'll get some great sunset shots," I said, gesturing over my shoulder. "When the sun breaks below that band of clouds, it's going to just ignite those buttes."

And it certainly would have. If the clouds had done what they were supposed to do. If I hadn't mistaken the edge of a secondary front that was developing for a local weather phenomenon. Instead, what happened was that the wind swung around 180 degrees in about .003 seconds and came blasting out of the north, turning instantly colder.

We scrambled to collect our things. Managed to collapse and secure the chairs before they followed the eagle off the escarpment, and, with effort, cracked the wind-pinned back door to the van so that Linda and travel dogs Max and Raven could get under cover. Me? I ran to the driver's side (to make sure the parking brake was on), opened the door . . .

And you know, ever since that moment (the moment the wind tore the door from my hands), that driver's-side door has never seated itself properly. For the next two months, late-sleeping campers all over the prairies would be treated to the *creeeeekBANG* of that door opening.

When Seasons Collide

What Linda and I were experiencing wasn't exactly the textbook spring storm pattern, but it was still pretty classic. The warm spring weather we had enjoyed in Nebraska was getting hit in the flank by a powerful surge of winter air. We had, in fact, been watching the skirmish line from the bluffs.

When cold and warm air masses collide, the colder, heavier air hugs the ground, forcing the warm, moist air skyward. Cooling as it climbs, the tropical air condenses into clouds that produce rain (and stuff like hail, sleet, and snow, too). The boundary between the cold and warm air can actually be seen. The clouds draw a line in the sky. Meteorologists refer to it as the "frontal boundary" or "squall line."

When the difference in air pressure between the two weather systems is great, as is often the case in spring, the resulting turbocharged weather has another label—a "frontal thunderstorm." This is a storm capable of producing large amounts of heavy rain in a short period of time, high winds, hail, and, in the most extreme cases, tornadoes—the dark and sinister side of spring on the prairies.

That's when clouds turn violent, spinning energy into a dark, writhing vortex that whips across the landscape with a wind force exceeding any other known weather event.

Not that we were overly concerned about tornadoes. We were, after all, outside the watch area. But it sure was windy. And it sure was weird how that front backed up on us.

BACK TO THE FRONT
As we made dinner, and the van rattled and rocked under the force of the wind, we watched the sky show un-

fold. Watched as the wall of clouds darkened, dropped, and showed incisor-shaped edges, as menacing as shark teeth.

Oddly, the clouds continued to move west, blocking the sunset and bringing on an early nightfall. Over dinner, overlooking the violence enveloping Pawnee Buttes, we watched as two migrating great blue herons climbed above the rim, and, though they were facing north, they were heading south.

To the east, the thunderheads went from white to pink to angry red, and in the south, distant lightning disclosed the outline of a particularly violent storm in molten moments. Conversation in the van went something like this.

"You think we'll be all right here tonight?"

"I think so. Hard to find someplace better in the dark."

"The van's bucking around a lot. Do you think the luggage carrier on top can take this wind?"

"Sure. We've had this thing up to eighty on the highway. The wind's not going to top that."

"Yeah, but we've never done eighty miles per hour backing up. The van's facing the wrong way, and the luggage carrier is blunt side to the wind."

"Oh. Yeah. Well, it will be all right. At least it's not snowing."

I don't know how hard the wind was blowing on the edge of that front and along the rim of the escarpment. All I know is that when we let Raven out to attend to business, she didn't leap back into the van—when her feet left the ground, she flew.

Later, around midnight, when I stepped outside to commune with the universe, the wind was blowing strong enough to move me off my feet, and the wind chill made "hurry" a compelling strategy.

The clouds were low, mostly unbroken but showing patches of moonlight where the wind stropped them thin.

"Don't worry," I said to the sleepy form that was my wife, "no precip."

Gauging by the quarter inch of ice that encased the van come morning, the rain, which then turned to sleet and snow, couldn't have started long after that premature pronouncement was made.

Dawn disclosed a Pawnee Grassland encased in a layer of gray ice and winds unabated. Over breakfast—as the last of the storm's sleet peppered the back of the van under gray skies in twenty-seven-degree temperatures—we listened to National Public Radio's weather reporter out of Fort Collins discuss the two inches of snow he'd dusted off his car. A "little bit of a surprise this morning" is how he referred to it and the blown prediction.

Denver received off-and-on snow all day, which screwed up both rush hours. But the story that dominated the news was the tornado in the town of Holly. Two hundred miles to the south, while Linda and I were having dinner on the Buttes, an F2 tornado tore through the small Prowers County border town, destroying sixty homes and killing a twenty-nine-year-old mother of two. The storm, according to the story in *The Pueblo Chieftain*, "defied forecasters' predictions." It struck the town at 8:00 P.M., shortly after the "severe thunderstorm advisory" for the region expired. It was a tragic but understandable mistake. The "dry line" between the cold and warm weather systems was expected to keep moving east, as fronts commonly do. It didn't. For reasons of its own, and in defiance of accepted logic, the line between seasons, weather systems, and, this time, life and death, shifted west.

Prowers County was where Linda and I were headed.

CHAPTER 4
The Empire Strikes Back

EMPIRE OF GRASS

Slightly more than two hundred years ago, in 1804, when Captains Meriwether Lewis and William Clark set off to secure America's claim to the vast and largely unexplored area recently purchased from France, they discovered a landscape creased by rivers and dotted with islands of trees. But in the main, almost incomprehensible in scale and scope, was a world ruled by grass. It is the near-perfect plant organism, well suited to withstand the rigors of the land.

Drought tolerant, grass thrives where average rainfall is insufficient to support the water-profligate needs of most tree species. Living tinder, grass is born to burn. Fire is one of the principal ecological forces on the prairies, and grasses, with most of their body mass rooted underground, are well adapted to a fire-driven environment.

Normal grazing poses no hardship, either. Clip a blade of grass, and the plant grows back. Able to suffer desertlike heat in the summer; adapted to Arctic conditions in winter; almost impervious to biped trespass (many early explorers commented on the remarkable property of prairie grass to spring back after being trod upon), grass is one tough plant. Enduring, too! When early explorers reached the prairies, the Age of Grass had lasted about eight thousand years.

This thriving prairie ecosystem, or biome, supported an array of animal species, most apparent of which were about seventy-five thousand native people (Clark estimated half this total); between 30 and 40 million bison, approximately 35 million pronghorn antelope, and the Great Spirit only knows how many prairie dogs. Estimates range from 200 million to 5 billion "barking squirrels," as Captain Lewis called them.

John James Audubon preferred the name "prairie marmot."

It takes a lot of grass to support this many grass-dependent species (although native America's, like the indigenous and now-extirpated prairie wolf and plains grizzly, are more accurately accounted among the ranks of secondary consumers—eating not grass but grass-eating animals). And there was a lot of grass—approximately 1.2 million square miles. The borders of the prairies extended north to the boreal forests of Alberta, Saskatchewan, and Manitoba;

south to the deserts of the American Southwest and the Hill Country of Texas; east to the limits of the eastern deciduous forest (reaching the Mississippi River in Iowa and Missouri), and west to the Rocky Mountains. An area about one third the size of the Lower Forty-eight states and larger than Mexico.

Lewis and Clark, on their voyage up the Missouri to the Pacific Ocean, saw only a fraction of this landscape. They were nevertheless impressed. But Thomas Jefferson's emissaries were not the first people of European descent to enter the prairies, and Lewis and Clark's sense of wonder was not universally shared.

In 1540, Francisco Vásquez de Coronado set off from Mexico City in the direction of present-day Kansas in search of gold. What he and his thousand-man contingent discovered instead was a "wilderness . . . of very small plants" and a landscape so open and fathomless that it stirred disquiet in their European souls. Back in 1803, when the merits of the proposed Louisiana Purchase were being debated in the halls of Congress, the always-eloquent Daniel Webster referred to the prairie real estate as "deserts of shifting sands and whirlwinds of dust." In somewhat like mind, the soldier-explorer Zebulon Pike compared it with the African Sahara. Even the great frontiersman and painter of wildlife John James Audubon described the Dakota scenery as "the most arid and dismal you can conceive of."

That Audubon was, as he made this observation, stuck on a Missouri River sandbar might have influenced his perspective; nevertheless, for much of the nineteenth century, the image of the "Great American Desert" was firmly (and perhaps not inaccurately) entrenched in the minds of Americans. Westward expansion exploded during this period. Wagon routes bearing famous names such as the Santa Fe Trail, the Oregon Trail, and the Mormon Trail ferried tens of thousands of foreign immigrants and gumption-spurred (or simply displaced) eastern residents to areas of fertile promise in California and Oregon, bypassing "No Man's Land," as the prairies were called.

On my wall, at home in New Jersey, is a map of the United States that once instilled geographic acumen in the minds of students in a schoolroom in Cape May. Published in 1851, it shows an America east of the Mississippi that would be familiar to all but West Virginia residents and bears a passing resemblance to what western residents are familiar with today. California was a state. So were Texas, Missouri, Iowa, Arkansas, and Louisiana.

Lying between the Rockies and those Mississippi River bordering states, are "territories" (like Kansas and Nebraska) and the "frontier," an extensive region colored appropriately yellow (like winter grass). Romantic images of westward expansion notwithstanding, America's last frontier was not the Far West. It was the geographic middle that pioneers hurriedly bypassed to get someplace else. Someplace that could support life.

But the prairies didn't remain the "frontier," or retain the name "desert," for long. Before, during, and especially just following the Civil War, they succumbed to a combination of pioneer spirit and good ol' American marketing.

Several social, political, and technological changes transpired in the late nineteenth century that altered both our
perception of the prairies and the face of the prairies themselves. The first was the removal of competition—princi-
pally the native people who had immigrated to the region,
from Asia, at least eleven thousand years ago and who, despite strong resistance, were nevertheless forced to surrender much of their land through a combination of military
pressure and a government-sanctioned campaign to eliminate the buffalo herds, which were the foundation of the native people's society and lives. This internment of Native
Americans on reservations opened the door for a new wave
of immigrants, mostly of American and European descent,
to supplant them.

But genocide was an attending objective, not the direct
cause of the great slaughter visited upon the vast herds of
buffalo that once roamed the prairie. Hunting for hides, for
select parts, and for sport had a cumulative impact. However
it was done, the destruction of the American bison eliminated a key component of the prairie ecology (almost as ecologically significant as drought, wind, and fire). The last free-
roaming prairie bison were effectively gone by 1880.

But even before the last nail in the bison's coffin was
hammered home, the door—make that gate—had already
opened for a new form of prairie exploitation, this by other
grass-loving ungulates, natives of Asia, refined in Europe,
and introduced to the American grasslands. These were
cattle. The introduction of cattle ushered in the age of the

open-range cowboys and, to no small degree, the world's enduring love affair with the image of the American West.

The substitution of one herding, grass-eating ungulate for another was not, strictly speaking, disastrous to the prairie ecology. Both cattle and bison are browsing animals. Both are designed to clip, digest, and redeposit grass (which, given grass's high silica content, is no universal feat among the ranks of herbivores). Both, if allowed, will move on from browsed areas to areas offering greater opportunity.

But cattle are less sun tolerant and more water dependent than bison. They also have a taste for forbs and shrubs, whereas bison are more grass-centric. Thirst and taste prompt cattle to focus more browsing effort in riparian woodlands (which commonly suffer from such attention), and their different pruning habits mean that the prairies have undergone, to some degree, an ecological, herbaceous shift. These differences, from an ecological standpoint, are a small matter.

It is what happened after the cattlemen that truly and dramatically altered the face of the prairies: agriculture arrived on the scene. First, in the more rain-soaked eastern and northern prairies—the tallgrass prairies. Later, in the higher, drier, western and southern mixed and shortgrass prairies. This agricultural expansion was, for the most part, a disaster. It was . . .

A WORLD TURNED UPSIDE DOWN
Grasslands are not grasslands for nothing. Across the planet, they occur in soil-based inland areas where moun-

tain ranges impede the passage of moisture-laden air and where temperatures and growing seasons are conducive to grasses. Given more water, most temperate landscapes will respond by producing forests. Given extremely cold and dry conditions, you get tundra. Hot and dry conditions beget deserts.

So climate fosters and supports grasslands. Fire and grazing animals maintain them. In the latter half of the nineteenth century, a new ecological force hit the prairies: farmers. They were armed with the steel plow (developed in 1837 by John Deere), which could cut through eight thousand years of fibrous crust, and barbed wire, "the devil's rope," which could protect cropland from the marauding of cattle (and in the process kill the age of open range).

These "sodbusters" arrived via a network of railroads that courted and cultivated a wave of immigration, then ferried (for a price) Russians, Germans, Scandinavians, and Scots to their very own corners in the Land of Opportunity. Homesteaders were encouraged by a government that passed a series of legislative acts, beginning with the Homestead Act of 1862, offering homesteaders 160-acre (later 640-acre) parcels at prices and terms that almost anyone could afford.

The only problem was that "vast" is not the same as "limitless." By the time John Frémont ran his presidential campaign under the slogan "Free Soil, Free Men, Frémont," there wasn't much good prairie land left in the Land of Opportunity. In fact, by the late 1800s, the only place left for latecomers to the American Dream was the much decried

Great American Desert. "Miles to water, miles to wood, six inches to hell," as the cowboys who had preceded the sod-busters might have told, and did tell, settlers. But the railroads and land speculators were singing a different song and promising a different land, a virtual Eden. "Rain follows the plow" was their promotional come-on, and what hundreds of thousands of hopeful, ambitious, and land-hungry immigrants wanted to hear.

And so they came, by the tens of thousands. And they plowed, turning the grass wrong side down. Exposing hundreds of thousands of acres of prairie soil that had not felt the desiccating touch of the sun or the driving force of the wind in eight thousand years. And sometimes rain did seem to follow the plow. Because on the prairies there are years, in fact periods, when rains are adequate, crops flourish, and profits can be made.

But just as there are wet years, there are dry ones. And just as there are wet periods, there are long, heartbreaking strings of years in which the skies are not cloudy all day and, contrary to the words of the old song, "discouraging words" and tumbleweed, a nonnative species also known as Russian thistle, are about the only things that do flourish.

THE GATHERING STORM

So in the late 1800s they came to the High Plains, the short-grass prairies, the "American Desert" (because that was all the free land that was left). They homesteaded. They turned the soil. And while some of these pioneers made it, many did not. The 1870s and 1890s were dry times. Crops withered. Homesteaders packed up, cut their losses, and moved out. But if the homesteaders were daunted, the promoters and profiteers were not.

More sodbusters arrived, and in the first decade of the new century, in southeastern Colorado, rainfall totals exceeded the sixteen inches per year average seven out of ten years—plenty enough rain to turn a profit. During the decade that saw the world mustering for war, wheat prices were sky high (over two dollars a bushel) and rainfall was, for the most part, adequate. More homesteaders arrived, driven by promise and profit. More land went under the plow.

In the 1920s, everything seemed to come together. Rainfall was mostly bountiful, and at no time were there two consecutive years when totals fell below average. Wheat prices remained high. The economy in the prairies, as elsewhere in the United States, was booming. Towns seemed to sprout out of the prairies overnight, serving the needs of a burgeoning and economically flush prairie population.

Farmers turning profits invested in equipment, particularly tractors and the "one-way plow," allowing them to strip ever more grass from the land even faster. Many had to, because now there were payments to be met, on land acquired with the help of the bank and loans on the equipment that made it economically feasible to farm those newly added acres.

Then, in the late twenties, the world grain market faltered. Grain backed up on the docks, in ships, in storage.

Prices for a bushel of grain plummeted, dipping below a dollar, then seventy-five cents! But the financial obligations didn't change, and mortgage payments didn't adjust with the economy. And all it took was simple math to see the economic solution. If prices in 1929 were only a third of what they'd been when you mortgaged the farm, then you had to plant three times as much land to make up the difference. So even more sod was busted, just to break even. And even more grain was grown, which was then piled atop the surplus in an already glutted market.

And then, on October 29, 1929, the stock market crashed. When 1930 saw record wheat harvests, it hardly mattered. With so much wheat sitting in storage, who was buying? Then, in 1931, when it looked like things could hardly get worse for prairie homesteaders, they absolutely and most certainly did.

Mother Nature began to take it all back. Just like the range-riding cowboys had prophesied, when the farmers peeled away the prairies, they took the wraps off of hell.

A Biome Too Far

The history of our species, and the planet, has largely been one of habitat alteration and exploitation. The Fertile Crescent, the cradle of agriculture, would not have earned this name but for the creative manipulation of water—a practice we call "irrigation." In Merry Old England, and across Europe, great forests were once the dominant vegetation—or did you think that the old fables Hansel and Gretel and Little Red Riding Hood were just tales? No, there really were forests where wolves prowled and maybe even where witches ensnared wayward children. But you can't eat trees. And they get in the way of crops. So the forests were cut. Land was cleared. Farm fields and pastures came to dominate the European landscape—and, to a large degree, continue to do so today.

We did much the same across the eastern United States. In fact, cutting the old-growth forest and turning it into agricultural land became something of a religious crusade in the late 1700s and early 1800s, and when Manifest Destiny reached the prairies, its history was almost past written. Altering the prairie habitat to meet our agrarian ambitions was just the newest chapter in a story going back thousands of years.

This chapter, however, was different. This time nature pushed us back, initiating (but not creating!) what must rank as the greatest ecological disaster in American history.

So far.

The 1930s in America were a bleak time all around, but for the people of the southern High Plains—particularly those living in southwestern Nebraska, southeastern Colorado, western Kansas, extreme eastern New Mexico, the Oklahoma Panhandle, and the Texas Panhandle, they were the darkest of times, too. Literally.

This was the Dust Bowl. The place where a prolonged but predictable drought, hubris, and foolish farming practices combined to shatter lives, the economy, and the ecology of a region. Even now, more than sixty years after rain finally returned to the land, the region has yet to recover fully.

In quick sum, what happened was this. Almost a million acres of land had been stripped of the protective covering that held the soil in check. Extreme drought and the moribund economy made agriculture futile, so crops were never planted. The land went fallow. With no ground cover, natural or planted, there was nothing to prevent the prairie wind from bearing the fine, dry, pulverized matter aloft and blowing it down the throats (and into the eyes, ears, and lungs) of everyone and everything in its path.

By the way, for much of this dust, hitching a ride on the wind was a practiced maneuver. Following the Ice Age, receding glaciers exposed unmeasured tons of fine, pulverized rock, which was borne aloft by ferocious winds coming off the ice sheets. This was the first Dust Bowl, witnessed perhaps by early aboriginal peoples, and it probably made the "Dirty Thirties" look like a second-string effort.

The thirties were horrible enough. When rains finally returned to the High Plains, in the 1940s, they fell upon a near-lunar landscape. One in which agriculture was moribund, the population was down to about two thirds of pre–Dust Bowl figures, and only the toughest towns were still functioning.

One of them was Lamar, Colorado.

Chapter 5
Lamar, Colorado

When the average traveler studies a map of Colorado, the eye is quickly drawn to the gratifyingly green wash that dominates the middle of the state, highlighting the splendor of the Rocky Mountains. The yellow-tinted urban centers of the Front Range—Fort Collins, Denver, and Colorado Springs—are equally eye-catching. Then things get visually vague.

If you study the big white expanse lying east of the Front Range, at first you find precious little. No tourist-friendly green, no urban centers; only two bold blue east-west-running highways that lead, as interstates are designed to do, somewhere else. But if you can recalibrate your expectations before your eyes follow the interstates off the page into Kansas and Nebraska, you will discover that this eastern third of the state is not featureless. It is divided into a grid of secondary roads, printed in capillary red, running for the most part north and south, east and west. Where these lines intersect, there are towns.

At one such intersection, the junction of U.S. Highways 50 and 287, is the town of Lamar, Colorado. Elevation 3,622 feet. Population 8,623. If you take the entire population of Prowers County (of which Lamar is the county seat), you find a mustering of about 14,000 souls. Divide this figure by the 1,646 square miles that constitute the county and you come up with a population density of 8.5 persons per square mile. If you do this same equation using cattle instead of people, you come up with 10 cows per square mile.

That's right. This is cattle and farm country. Has been, in fact, since Lamar, Colorado, was located on Section 31, Township 22, Range 46 on May 24, 1886. Back then, this section of U.S. Highway 50 was better known as the Santa Fe Trail.

Location now, as then, is everything, and it goes a long way toward explaining why it is that Lamar survived as a retail and industrial base serving southeastern Colorado when so many other towns succumbed to the Depression, the Dust Bowl, and the slow, erosive friction of a hard environment that left lesser prairie communities high and dry. Located along the banks of the Arkansas River and the old

Santa Fe Trail, the town benefited early from overland travel and commerce to California. Since the 1994 North American Free Trade Agreement, the lines of commerce have increasingly run north and south—with goods crossing into the United States from Texas ports of entry and trucked into the northern prairies via Route 287.

The town itself is named after Lucius Quintus Cincinnatus Lamar, who served as President Grover Cleveland's secretary of the interior. No, he wasn't a native son—he never set foot in Prowers County. But he was the official in charge of determining where federal land offices were to be situated, and local leaders speculated he'd be favorably disposed toward designating the town that bore his name. The coveted land office did indeed come to Lamar, but whether flattery figured into the decision is anyone's guess.

Today, Lamar boasts two FM radio stations (one oldies, one country and western), a truck stop, a state police barracks, a Super Wal-Mart, twenty-five churches, seven bars, two pawnshops, and an assortment of banks, stores, and eating places. The ratio of churches to bars is noteworthy when you consider that Lamar was once frisky enough to employ the talents of lawmen like Bat Masterson to keep order. As a matter of historic fact, six saloons were established by the end of the town's first week of incorporation. It was more than a month before the first church service was held here.

Today, *The Lamar Ledger*'s "Police Report" is dominated by traffic incidents, responses to security system false alarms, and responses to conflicts and disputes in which the tersely written accounts often end with the observation that "no further action was taken." Pretty tame stuff compared with the violence that dominates the pages of newspapers emanating from Front Range urban centers.

Did I mention that William Jennings Bryan visited Lamar in 1912? So did the silver screen cowboy personality Tom Mix, who, in his days before stardom, boasted to reporters of once having worn a law officer's badge in the nearby town of Two Buttes. It is interesting that he is remembered locally only as having been employed as a bartender.

But hyperbole and loquaciousness are the exceptions in this part of the world, where to be born here is the norm and to vote anything but Republican is not. (In fact, if Colorado is a traditional "red state," Prowers County is probably closer to the maroon end of the political spectrum.) But in Lamar, you can pretty much count on people to be honest, direct, and comfortable in a world where values are a matter of fact, not debate.

If you want to know what's going on in Lamar, Prowers County, you can ask Chana Reed at the Chamber of Commerce or Mary Breslin, editor of *The Lamar Ledger*—and you will find, as I did, that they are forthright and helpful. But if you want the real dirt, the place to go is the Hickory House Restaurant on I-50. There, every morning, sometimes even before the door is open to the public at 5:30, the town worthies caucus to discuss the weighty matters of the world. It's where Linda and I went to get the first and last word on spring.

I'm saddened to tell you that, in A.D. 2007, you must go ten, sometimes twenty miles off the interstate to find vessels of wisdom and regional culture like the Hickory House. They call it a restaurant, but it is, in reality, an American institution known as a café, to which all-night truckers drive an hour past hunger in anticipation of steak and eggs, then dawdle for coffee and cream pie; where locals are greeted by their first names; and where the appearance of morning regulars is interrupted only by sickness or death.

Interstate highways have sucked the life out of places where towns have the poor fortune to be I-flanked. Fifty years after Dwight David Eisenhower's transportation vision was cast in asphalt, you can find the boarded-up shells of once-thriving main-street cafés, some with yellowing signs still taped to the windows advertising the last come-on breakfast special. They lie within earshot of the interstate and often within sight of the easy-on, easy-off enterprises that killed them: places like McDonald's, Burger King, Cracker Barrel, Flying J, and other familiar icons of epicurean and cultural homogenization.

Hickory House was spared. U.S 270, a major north-south trucking route, runs past, not around, its door. And while the usual array of fast-food joints have established themselves in Lamar, Hickory House's popularity has not flagged. Maybe it's the pie. More likely it's the atmosphere and the conversation—not that as an outsider you are necessarily privy to this.

Shadow. Dawn, Groundhog Day, Pawnee National Grassland, Colorado. By all the signs, six more weeks of winter on the American prairies. At minus fifteen degrees, you can bet the smile is frozen on my face.

ABOVE: *A sample of the wealth of sandhill cranes on the Platte River in April.*

LEFT: *Several adult sandhill cranes rest and have a drink at a bar on the Platte River.*

RIGHT: *Welcome to the town of Milnesand, lesser prairie-chicken capital of New Mexico. Shown here, about half the town.*

BELOW: *A male lesser prairie-chicken booming on a lek. It's the sound of spring on the prairies.*

Two male lesser prairie-chickens determining which bird has the "right stuff." The females are judging from the sideline.

ABOVE: *Prairie dog holes and burrowing owls. Perfect together.*

BELOW: *Earth Day on the Comanche Grassland with my civic-minded friend Johnny Earth Day. As you can see from the refuse-free landscape, he does good work.*

ABOVE: *The pool in Picture Canyon. Too late. If you've traveled this far into the canyon, the place has already cast a spell on you.*

BELOW: *If pictographs could talk, what a story of early settlement in southeastern Colorado this one could tell.*

ABOVE: *Just another prairie sunrise. Maybe you'll catch the next one.*

RIGHT: *A red-tailed hawk demonstrates a perfect launch from one of its favorite perches. Even the Russian judge would award this one a 9.5.*

ABOVE: *A morning blessed with a bumper crop of morning glories. Time to savor.*

LEFT: *They look delicate, but morning glories are tough grassland plants—ideally suited for life in the windy, desiccating open.*

ABOVE: *In May, while many other prairie birds are just setting up house, the early-breeding horned lark already has young to feed.*

RIGHT: *Shy and increasingly uncommon, mountain plover are birds of the high prairies, despite the name.*

OPPOSITE: *A male lark bunting, the state bird of Colorado, announcing that this perch is his, and your perch, Mr. Rival Male, is somewhere else.*

ABOVE: *A swift fox, a prairie specialist, enjoys the warmth of a strong spring sun near the entrance to its den in the Pawnee Grassland.*

RIGHT: *A western meadowlark celebrates spring with song.*

OPPOSITE: *Another spring storm on the prairies. No place to run. Few places to hide.*

LEFT: *Pronghorn are very fast, but they can also be very curious.*

BELOW: *A female bison, who has seen lots of Custer State Park tourists in her time, and her calf, who apparently has not.*

ABOVE: *A black-tailed prairie dog suing for peace. Once abundant almost beyond reckoning, populations have been hit hard by loss of habitat, persecution by ranchers, and outbreaks of plague.*

BELOW: *No, Custer isn't buried here, and neither are the remains of many of the Seventh Cavalry soldiers who were killed at the Little Bighorn. Their remains are now part of the prairie ecosystem. What they fought and died for, they became.*

Journeys, like seasons, end. But when one season ends, another begins. It's the same with adventures.

The town's Worthies sit in the southwest corner of the building—next to the two-pot coffeemaker and well away from the counter and booths. Weighty matters, openly discussed, demand privacy, and the waitresses, who are the caucus's facilitators, carefully direct breakfastgoers away from the corner table.

The Worthies, as is their privilege, simply walk past the "Please wait to be seated" sign and take their customary chairs.

A quorum for Lamar's morning think tank is about eight, and on the morning when Linda and I first sat down for pancakes and bacon, the corner table was full. Outside it was cold and windy, and the snowpack, left over from the winter's multiple blizzards, still blanketed the ground.

The caucus's members are generally older, mostly retirees who are able to bring a variety of avocational disciplines to bear on items on the agenda. Since they are retired, they enjoy the latitude to direct all the time and attention that is needed when dealing with some of the world's most sensitive issues. Issues like

Water rights! Certainly the most hotly debated subject in the West. King Solomon's sword couldn't apportion justice on this one, but if there is a solution to be had, you can bet the Worthies already have it packaged, with a ribbon on it, and could have sent it to Congress several times over (if only they'd been asked).

The Academy Awards. The morning we were there, *An Inconvenient Truth*'s award for Best Documentary set off a whole coffeepot's worth of discussion relating to global warmi——make that climate change.

And, of course, the weather commands no small measure of attention. People who live on the prairies see a lot of it, and much of what they see falls in the range of extremes. If the weather is so much a part of daily conversation, it is because it affects their lives so much.

The caucus members aren't big fans of Oprah. Apparently she once stayed at the Best Western's Cow Palace Inn, just down the street, and complained about the smell from the local feedlot. They do like baseball caps. Six of the caucus members were wearing caps. Only one wore a Stetson, and one standing member was bareheaded.

Wore caps while eating? Not necessarily. Some of the Worthies limit their morning intake to coffee.

And while from the far side of the restaurant matters under discussion are often heard only in snatches, there are some things listeners can garner that are perfectly and wonderfully clear. Laughter is full and honest, and makes up between half and two thirds of the discussion. And the voices themselves have in common that wonderful, visceral rumble that is endemic to the West. It's a sound that inspires confidence. And I tell you this, with no small measure of wonder, that no matter how delicate the discussion, no matter how hot the topic, the most expressive expletives that ever pass the edge of the table are *darn, shoot,* and *heck.*

Do you know of any other think tank dealing with high-stakes matters anywhere in the world that can boast a PG rating for language and content?

If the president ever needs to know how to fix the mess in the Middle East or deal with a nuclear Iran or bring all those fractious little countries in the United Nations to heel, he could just dispense with the cabinet and set up a hotline to the table where the Worthies caucus.

This is why I courted their counsel on our first visit, one windy day in late winter, on a question that was central to this book. I did this, I might add, with no small measure of trepidation. The Worthies set their own agenda. Noncaucus members introducing items onto the docket are almost certainly aberrations. Might, in fact, be unprecedented.

"Good morning, fellas," I said, trying my best not to sound like someone from New Jersey writing a book. "Mind if I ask a question?"

Their silence fell just short of rejection. Their fixed gaze said: "Go on."

"I'm here attending the town's Snow Goose Festival," I said, trying to buy a measure of confidence with some background and disclosure, "and I've been wondering. What's the first sign of spring in this country?"

The silence continued while the members, each in his own mind, considered first whether the question met procedural guidelines (asked, as it was, by a noncommittee member) and then, perhaps, whether it was within their jurisdiction, insofar as the seasons are in the domain of a higher order.

"Well," one of the Worthies intoned, "I think it's spring when th' firs' buds begin t' open."

"You kin aw'most hear them pop it happens so fast," another added.

I nodded, writing. Clearly it was a question each had considered on his own, whether or not it had been discussed in the general assembly. Clearly I'd come to the right place.

"An' birds singin'," another member suggested. "It's spring when the birds start singin'."

"Like robins?" I suggested.

"Like robins," he confirmed.

"When is that?" I asked.

"Why, the first day of spring," he said matter-of-factly.

That's why the president needs these men. Have that mess in the Middle East cleared up in no time.

BIRDING FOR HOLLY: GRANADA, COLORADO, APRIL 4, 5:00 A.M.

It was the only other vehicle in the Stop 2 Shop convenience store in Granada, Colorado, and while it wasn't the expected pickup truck, the Arena Dust Tours brand on the door and process of elimination suggested that the driver was . . .

"Fred?" I said to the 100 percent denim-clad figure fussin' (as they say in southeastern Colorado) with sumthin' inside the green SUV.

"Hullo?" he said, standing, turning, absorbing my hand more than taking it. Sized and contoured like a catcher's mitt, the rancher's hands had a banker's fleshiness, but when they enveloped my hand, it was plain that the palms had been cured by a lot of rough wood, hard metal, and strap leather and that the backs had seen a lot of sun. Working hands are not the exception in Prowers County. Farming and ranching are what people mostly do in these parts (unless they work in Lamar in stores or businesses that service the ranch and farming community). And Fred Dorenkamp—whose father homesteaded north of Cheyenne Wells in the 1920s and who grew up in a home where his mother lit lamps, at noon, to dispel the gloom cast by Dust Bowl storms—was a cattle rancher who later specialized in raising and delivering bucking broncs and bulls for the rodeo circuit.

Two of Fred's animals, Voodoo Skoal and Satan Skoal, may still haunt the dreams of surviving bull riders.

Now, for much of the year, he and his wife, Norma, are proprietors of Arena Dust Tours, a homegrown enterprise specializing in wildlife- and bird-watching tours. But from early April to early May, Fred is hired by the Colorado Division of Wildlife to survey lesser prairie-chickens in Prowers County. He's a chicken rider. Linda and I were going along for the ride.

Ten minutes later, while dawn was just entertaining the notion of illuminating the eastern sky, we were eastbound toward the Kansas line and hoped-for rendezvous with lesser prairie-chickens.

Chicken Little

North America boasts nineteen native game bird species. Some are forest birds, some are tundra birds, some are birds of mixed grass and woodlands or desert areas, but two are pure prairie specialists. They don't like deserts. They don't much like trees (not tall ones, anyway). They like prairie. Hence the name, prairie-chicken. And once, they were as common as the prairies were extensive. Now, they are as uncommon as the prairies are limited.

The more widespread of the two, the greater prairie-chicken, once ranged from the grasslands of coastal Texas north into the Canadian prairies and east into Ontario, Ohio, Kentucky, and northern Tennessee. Today, it is found in only seven states. A distinct subspecies with a disjunct population called the "heath hen" once ranged from northern Virginia to eastern Massachusetts and survived long enough to embrace extinction in 1932, in the same century that saw the demise of the last passenger pigeon.

But the lesser prairie-chicken, while once numerous, has always been more geographically restricted, found only in southeastern Colorado, southern and western Kansas, extreme eastern New Mexico, western Oklahoma, and north-central Texas. It still exists in these states, in numbers that may generously be called vestigial. Since the 1800s, the population has declined by over 95 percent. More alarmingly, since the mid-sixties, the range has decreased by nearly 80 percent. This gives the lesser prairie-chicken the distinction of being the grouse with the smallest and the most restricted population in North America.

Hence the need for chicken riders to keep tabs on the numbers.

Most of the leks that serve as the booming grounds for breeding males in spring are found on private land, and landowners, as a rule, are not partial to strangers. They're even less tolerant of people who work for the government—state or federal.

Hence the need for local, rancher-friendly chicken riders like Fred.

First Contact

We turned off a paved road onto a graded county road that led to another county road that led to a rutted tract across open grassland. Fred came to a stop. "We should be able to hear them from here," he explained.

Stepping onto grass sparkling with frost and the first light of morning, we cupped our hands behind our ears and listened. Sure enough, on the facing hill, we could just make out the sound of booming males.

Booming, by the way, is something of a misnomer—or perhaps a window to a bygone era, when birds were abundant and the din of males on the lek approached the level of torture. The vocalization commonly made by displaying males "sounds like a coffee percolator," our practical guide suggested. "When I first started doin' this, I thought I was supposed to be listenin' for somethin like a sonic boom." The memory brought a chuckle from Prowers County's chicken specialist. The rancher and buckin' bronc breeder Dorenkamp got his job as chicken rider by attending a meeting and being solicited by a regional biologist with the

Colorado Division of Wildlife. Said Fred, with a muffled laugh, "I never in a million years thought I'd be doing sumthin' like this. I always liked birds but . . ."

It was light enough now to see features, and I could finally see Fred's. A big man with an easy, ambling bearing, he looks like a cross between Tip O'Neill and Norman Schwarzkopf and every once in a while flashes a smile worthy of Dwight David Eisenhower. But now he was concentrating, not smiling.

"Let's git over to the other side so we have the sun to our backs," he directed.

Four, Two, and One

I couldn't figure out how Fred was maneuvering in what was, to my eyes, flat and featureless terrain, but I've seen boat captains, on the open sea, navigate with similar skill. Sure enough, five minutes later the light was behind us and the sound of booming birds in front.

"Do you see any yet?" he asked. I didn't. But I could sure hear them. Close. Coming from the flat, grassy area.

"There," I directed. Just to the right of the moon. "Saw a bird jump. Just hold this course."

"Dang," said Fred. "Yesterday they was back up that hill." What hill? I thought.

We eased forward, closing to within seventy yards of the birds.

"I don't want to go any closer. 'Fraid to spook 'em," said our guide. It didn't matter. We were close enough.

Close enough to see the clutch of four males comfortably

spaced in a formation about the size and shape of a baseball diamond. All of the birds had their plum-colored air sacs inflated. All were leaning forward. All had their hornlike pinnae erect and projecting.

They looked like feathered bulls leaning forward into some invisible matador's cape. They seemed as tense and focused as infielders on a three-and-two-count pitch. But unlike that of birds playing in the infield, their attention was not on the dueling males in the center of the field— each facing the other from a distance of two feet, doing his level best to face the opponent down. No, they were focused on the single, all-brown lump of a bird that the growing light disclosed to be the single female sitting quietly not far from the dueling males.

"How many do you see?" asked Fred.

"Six males, one female," I replied.

"Had seven males yesterday," Fred noted.

"One male flew off as we were pulling up," I replied.

Maybe Fred nodded. I was busy watching the birds, the males doing their lofting, foot-pattering best to gain the female's attention (and her ardor).

The female? She was, by all appearances, indifferent. But this was just an appearance. She was there. On the booming ground. And this speaks for itself. Says, loud and clear: "I'm in the game. I'm playing the field. Now . . . who's got the right stuff? Who's big enough, quick enough, bold enough, burly enough, and good enough for me to mix my genes with?"

So let's see what you got, boys.

But we couldn't stick around long enough to see which of the players was going to score.

That's the problem with doing a survey. You've got to keep surveyin'.

BOOM AND BUST

The next site was last year's premier lek.

"Had seventeen males here, last year. Put the viewing blind so close, the birds was behind us."

The blind, a Division of Wildlife–supplied mobile trailer with built-in bleachers, was still in position. The birds were not. Maybe it was because of the early date. Maybe it was because of the spell of cool weather that seemed to have temporarily put the brakes on spring. But the unspoken fear was that the birds themselves had been hard hit by the winter storms that had dumped over forty inches of snow on the county, making international news. And it wasn't just the amount of snow that was so devastating. The blizzard's impact on wildlife was exacerbated because it came on the heels of an ice storm that "flattened things," followed by temperatures that didn't moderate.

The first snow to hit the region had fallen on December 20. But the big dump on the southeastern prairies didn't happen until the Friday before New Year's Day. That's when forty inches fell on Lamar, paralyzing the town for three days and forcing the Colorado National Guard into action to help ranchers find and airdrop feed to cattle stranded by the storm. They saved thousands. They lost thousands more—to the capping snowpack, unmerciful cold, and a third storm, which then dumped an additional fifteen inches of white misery on the region. Estimates by the Colorado Cattlemen's Association put the loss at ten to fifteen thousand head of cattle. Nobody calculated the loss to wildlife.

"The last of it didn't melt until nine days ago," Fred said with a shake of his head—a gesture that fell short of approximating the hardships associated with the storm.

One of the reasons Linda and I had chosen Lamar for our journey into spring was precisely the winter snowfall. Prowers County was in the sixth year of a drought. The snows, while disruptive and devastating, promised, at least, much-needed moisture for the soil.

Promised a prairie spring to remember.

Providing, of course, you were an antelope, jackrabbit, or prairie-chicken that survived to see it.

"Do you hear any?" Fred asked.

"No," I said. "Nothing but meadowlarks," I added.

"Been seein' lots fewer meda'larks this year, too," he said. "Might have to move that blind," he added with a shrug.

HOLLY

We drove to several other sites and found a few birds here and there. At the final location, a place that had gone from grass to farmland, we didn't find booming birds, but as we drove by, birds—three this time—flushed.

"I'm beginnin' to feel a little better," said Fred. The birds might not have been displaying, but the chicken rider was optimistic about the prospects for the birds and the breeding season that was just starting.

We were about to get a lesson in the meaning of opti-mism.

"That's Holly up ahead," he said, directing our attention toward the grain elevator towering over the cluster of trees ahead. "How 'bout sum breakfast? Then I'll show ya sum of the devastation."

Linda and I had talked about visiting Holly after learn-ing about the tornado. We weren't motivated by morbid cu-riosity or, worse, idle curiosity. But neither of us had ever seen the kind of damage a tornado can inflict, and the twister had touched the lives of the prairie residents we hoped to engage with this book. Perhaps some account should be included? A poignant footnote to the dark side of spring on the prairies?

We had decided against it, because in some small way we wanted to support the people whose lives had been so af-fected. The best way we could think of was honoring their privacy. But now we were with Fred, who lived here, and who seemed eager for us to see the damage the town had endured.

We came in on the east side of Holly, whether by design or because that is where Jack and Wanda's Tasty House Café just happens to be, I don't know. I only know that what we saw of the town before breakfast didn't dampen our ap-petites and that the atmosphere inside the café was friendly, almost casual—certainly nothing befitting a disaster area one week after the fact.

The mobile news vans were mostly gone, the hundreds of volunteers serving up meals disbanded.

Our impression changed after breakfast, when we continued west. We saw the scores of leveled houses. The mangled wreckage of cars. The trees and the lives and the town stripped of the promise of spring.

We tried not to stare, but you couldn't not stare. And as we attempted to comprehend the scale of the damage, we tried to concentrate while Fred offered personal accounts of the friend of his who lived "in this house here," and how the damage in "this 'n here" was only now becoming apparent, as it started to settle, and "do you see that two-bah-four sticking through that wall? That's my nephew's house, and if his son had been asleepin in his bed when that twister hit . . ."

Everyone said it was lucky that the storm struck at dinnertime, when people were alert, and not three hours later, when people would have taken to bed.

But what was most compelling, what was most affirming, was the activity coursing through the town. People in their yards and work crews in the streets, restoring order. Putting lives back in place.

Hardy people like Fred Dorenkamp, whose fathers and grandfathers and great-grandfathers had suffered the hardship of getting and settling here. Who'd survived the Dust Bowl. Who endure periodic droughts and world-class winter storms. Who get up the next morning and, from the strength they find within, and from the strength they draw from their friends and neighbors, get on with their lives.

If you are ever curious to know where the strength of this country comes from, you can drive to Holly, Colorado, and see for yourself. It is impressive. It is affirming.

And on one street, where most of the houses, while not undamaged, were still standing—just one block over from the street brought to a standstill by the hundreds of people who had come to the funeral of the tornado's only fatality—there was an untroubled patch of daffodils and tulips. They weren't there in defiance. They weren't there to make a statement. They weren't there for any other reason except that it was spring. Blooming is just what flowers do in the spring. They'll do it next year, too. And the prairie-chickens on their leks? With luck, they'll be there, too.

And the people of Holly? The sons and daughters of pioneers. What do you think?

PLAYING THE FIELD

The closing bars of the national anthem sent spectators in this corner of the land of the free and the home of the brave back to their seats and ballplayers running for their respective positions. The hosting La Junta High School Tigers (1 and 6 for the season) took the field. The visiting Lamar Savages (5 and 1) headed to the dugout and the batter's box. In front of the stands, several lawmen made their presence known and felt. While the likelihood of terrorist activities in La Junta is slim, the rivalry between Lamar and La Junta high schools is long and abiding. It is always easier to promote cordial relationships than to restore order.

Besides, who doesn't like to watch a baseball game?

On the mound for the Tigers, wearing number 8, was Tabor Weaver, a compact, square-faced, short-haired, serious young jock who looked like a future regional sales manager for John Deere. Facing him was Jordan Romine, number 12, a slender, pale-eyed figure with lots of curly blond hair billowing out from beneath a cap that he picked up off the ground after every pitch. He had the makings of a molecular biologist (if he applied himself), or the start-up founder of some culture-shifting industry based upon technology that has yet to be invented (if he did not).

What was I doing there? I was playing a hunch or, more accurately, making a point. Sure, baseball is almost synonymous with spring (never mind that players are referred to as the "Boys of Summer"). The smell of the grass, the sound of the crowd, the crack of the bat.

And in the field, nine lithe, loose, but altogether focused athletes. Bringing all their youthful vigor to bear, doing their best to do their best and show off the qualities that got them into their school uniforms (and the lettermen's club, and the yearbook team photo) and all the other tokens that distinguish them for the superior competitors that they are.

Speed. Strength. Quickness. Good eye-hand coordination. Brains.

If you're a young man with the right stuff, this is the place to show it. If you are a prospecting female, looking for the right stuff, this is the place to find it.

PLAY BIRD; PLAY BALL

Lamar got off to a slow start. Three up, three down. Tabor was throwing well.

Now on the mound, Jordan threw a few warm-up pitches while La Junta's lead-off batter did all the important things batters do to get ready for the duel. Kick up dirt. Spit on hands. Swing the bat menacingly two or three times. Lock eyes.

Have you ever watched bulls in a pasture, bison on the range, sumo wrestlers in the ring? They go through a ritual somewhat like this.

And it was at this point that I kind of lost interest in the game. It wasn't my focus anyway. What I was interested in was the biological foundation of competitive sports and, perhaps, the interactive dynamics. Because when you look at baseball, and you look at a prairie-chicken lek, you can't help but note the similarities.

Bunch of young males of the species all spread around on an easy-to-view, dirt and grass field with a high point (AKA mound) in the middle. Two (or more) rivals facing each other, head to head. Other males defending territories of their own from encroachment.

The batter swings. Connects with the ball. Sends it flying into the area between the center and left field. The batter doesn't want to hit it where outfielders are standing. That's their core territory, the place that's easiest for them to defend.

The center fielder signals "his ball." Can he catch it? Beat back the challenge? He'll do his best. And in the bleachers there are watching, measuring eyes.

High stakes.

A lesser prairie-chicken stands in the middle of his territory. A rival male encroaches on the periphery. Can the territorial bird beat back the challenge, face down his encroaching rival? He sure hopes so. His genes are counting on it. And on the periphery, the eyes of females are on him.

High stakes.

"Come on, Black," a fan shouts behind me. "Let's see some hustle out there."

"I've got to go over to the other side," I said to Linda.

"And leave me here?" she said, none too happily.

"I'll be back. I just need a different perspective."

By the way, the guys in black are Lamar. Unlike prairie-chickens, in baseball rival males have different plumages.

CLUTCH HITTERS

I mounted the bleachers on the La Junta side and took a seat offering an open view across the field. Trying not to appear too obvious, I trained my binoculars back into the ranks of "black" boosters seated in the visitor section. There were about two hundred Lamar fans, and it didn't take more than a glance to see that they were not randomly distributed.

Parents, grandparents, and regular boosters (i.e., former Lamar baseball greats who never grew up) were spread out over much of the lower and southern side of the bleachers. But up in the top north quadrant, away from the adults, were members of the student body—about seventy to eighty strong. Smack in the middle was what I was looking for. Four rows deep, six to eight across, was a clutch of single, unattached female viewers—about thirty in all. Just as on prairie-chicken leks, females tend to cluster. Watching. Waiting.

If you care to tell me that all these attentive young girls—who were, despite the chill, mostly unjacketed and wholly dressed for effect—were there because they just like baseball or wanted to show their school spirit, that's fine. I'm equally certain that young men play baseball, and football, and basketball, and run track and field because they like to get tired and sweat.

The fact remains, the boys of summer were in the field. The girls, in the stands, were watching the field. Moving one's genes ahead into the next generation is the most serious endeavor a species can engage in—no matter how evolved, no matter the particulars concerning the display or pairing mechanism. Compared with mating, everything else is just a game.

IT HAPPENS EVERY SPRING

Lamar had a big fourth inning. Scored seven runs off a hapless Tabor Weaver (who was pulled at the end of the fifth). The Lamar bats were just too much.

But the Tigers, down 7 to 1, staged a great comeback in the seventh. They filled the bases before a tiring Jordan Romine had to face down two more batters. He fanned the first. But got hit on by the second. Demonstrating reflexes that were nothing short of superb, and intelligence to boot, Jordan fielded the bouncing grounder himself and, ignoring the runner sprinting for home, threw the batter out at first.

Yay, Lamar!

On the field, the teams lined up for the ritual down-the-line handshakes. After all, it's not whether you win or lose, it's how you play the game.

It is just a game, after all.

In the stands, the moms and dads and grandparents and boosters were moving quickly for the parking lot. Beat the rush; get home for dinner. But in the top north corner, in the student section, there was less hurry. In fact, some of the young fans didn't move at all. They sat there watching. Waiting.

WHITE EASTER

"An upper-level weather system over western Utah will move south to the Four Corners region tonight, causing a moist southwest flow out ahead of the . . .

"At the same time upslope winds wrapping around a surface high-pressure system east of our region will bring moisture and cold air in from the east . . .

"At the same time a weak weather disturbance over northern Colorado will bring cold weather and moisture into the region . . .

"These three systems, and temperatures remaining nearly the same as last night, will continue the threat of . . ."

What this National Weather Service report meant was that it was snowing. Hard.

We were leaving Lamar, heading south on Highway 287, en route to the Comanche National Grassland. Traffic was understandably light. In addition to the poor driving conditions, it was April 8, Easter Sunday. If you aren't fishing, needing milk, or going to church, there is little reason to be out and about at 9:00 A.M. on Easter Sunday, and between Lamar and Springfield there are about as many places to worship as there are places to buy milk or wet a line.

These number zero.

We made it as far as Springfield, county seat for neighboring Baca County, before worsening conditions, coupled with a number of snow-covered vehicles approaching from the opposite direction, suggested a change of strategy.

"Let's head back to Two Buttes," I suggested.

"Oh, getting stuck in Two Buttes is much better than getting stuck in Carrizo Canyon," Linda observed.

"We won't get stuck," I assured her. "It's heading into the sixties tomorrow. Any snow accumulation will be gone by morning."

"And you are basing this assumption on what authority?" Linda invited, pointing at the thermometer display on the rearview mirror, which read thirty-one degrees. When we left Lamar, the temperature had been thirty-seven degrees.

"On NOAA Weather Radio."

Linda let silence and the long and checkered track record of the National Weather Service serve as an answer.

"Okay. Noon at the latest."

Silence.

"We can stop by that prairie dog town and see whether there are any burrowing owls out. Be a great shot. Owls in snow."

It would have been a great shot, but we'd overlooked one thing . . . make that three. Owls don't fish, don't run out of milk, and, as creatures who emerge from subterranean chambers routinely, are not overly impressed with Easter.

Happy First Sunday After the First Full Moon Following the Equinox

The snow was still heavy but mostly melting as it touched the ground when we reached Two Buttes. The winds, which had been blustery on the open plains, were down to zephyr force in the canyon.

"Want to go for a walk?" I invited.

"Love to, sweetie," Linda replied, "but I've got two days of images to go through." Translation: "No, I don't want to get wet and cold. Are you nuts?"

"Walk?" I encouraged our canine companions.

The ensuing pupalanche made it as far as the door. Stopped. Retreated. Max and Raven opted to help Linda edit photos. Given the less-than-springlike weather, it would have been a very good morning to be in church, observing Christianity's most important holiday, and, if truth be known, that had been our original plan. To join the townspeople of Lamar in their Easter celebration at one of the twenty-five, or so, Christian places of worship.

Which denomination? It hardly mattered. The denominational spin was less important than the celebration itself and its religious foundation—the epic drama of life (meaning light, meaning warmth, meaning spring) surmounting death (meaning cold, meaning darkness, meaning winter). In the end, Linda and I had decided to cut out the middlemen and just buy direct—i.e., celebrate the pageant outdoors.

Churches may indeed be divinely inspired. And the Easter story is central to both Christianity and the Easter celebration. But in case you have never heard it, in quick sum, Jesus of Nazareth, prophet and promised savior, journeys to Jerusalem to celebrate the Jewish Passover and fulfill prophecy and his destiny. He is betrayed by one of his followers. Arrested and condemned for heresy by the Romans. Tortured. Humiliated. Executed and buried.

End of story? No. The beginning of a new religion. On the morning of the third day, a loyal band of female followers go to the tomb and discover, to their astonishment, that the tomb is empty.

He has risen. As ordained by prophecy.

It's life defeating death. It's renewal incarnate.

That is the Easter story. But the Easter celebration we know today is actually a hybrid of pagan custom and ancient religions, whose common denominator is the celebration of spring—the return of the world to light and warmth after three months of cold and darkness.

What's not to celebrate? Well, on this particular Easter Sunday, the weather for one thing. I headed down the road in an easterly direction, not for any religious or literary reasons but because that way the snow wouldn't be blowing in my face.

If you wanted to pick a perfect season to celebrate the resurrection of a Messiah, you couldn't do much better than
spring. Interestingly enough, this is pretty much what
happened. As just recounted, Jesus was crucified on the
eve of the Jewish Passover, and on the third day he rose
from the dead. A dispute within the early Christian
church arose between those who wanted to hold to the
Jewish Passover timeline and celebrate the Resurrection
following the Passover celebration (the position espoused
by Eastern Christians) and those who insisted that the celebration of the Resurrection should always fall on a Sunday (the choice of Western or Roman Christians).

In A.D. 325 the Roman Emperor Constantine I convoked
the Council of Nicaea, where it was decided that Easter
would henceforth be celebrated on the first Sunday following the first full moon following the vernal equinox.

Now you know why Easter falls on a different date each
year and is, as the expression goes and the lunar cycle dic-
tates, a "movable feast."

The emperor's edict didn't entirely solve the problem.
Eastern churches balked (to this day their celebration commonly falls a week before or after the date celebrated by
Western churches), and while the emperor's formula might
have been adopted, the absence of a universally accepted
calendar undermined universal conformity. It wasn't until
1582 and adoption of the Gregorian calendar that everyone
was finally on the same (calendar) page, and Easter Sunday

was Easter Sunday everywhere in the Western world. That's not the point.

The point is that the fixed point of reference for Christians' holiest holiday is not the day their savior rose from the dead. It is the vernal equinox! The first day of spring! The same date chosen by scores of earlier (i.e., pagan) religions and cultures to hold their celebrations of fertility and rebirth.

It gets better (or worse, depending upon your religious point of view). Many of Easter's most familiar icons, like the Easter Bunny (a symbol of fertility) and the Easter egg, also have their roots in the pagan past. Even the name, Easter, has a pagan origin. According to the Venerable Bede, writing in the early eighth century, the name derives from Eoestre, the Druid goddess of spring, to whom the month of April is dedicated (in fact, her name comes from the Saxon word for spring, *eastre*). It was common practice for the early Christian ministry to market their new religion by grafting Christian celebrations onto older established ones.

Remember the Imbolc (i.e., Groundhog Day) celebration and Candlemas Day?

The prime example of holiday co-option is the celebration of Christ's birth, or Christmas, which was superimposed over pagan celebrations of the winter solstice, despite the fact that most historians fix the actual birth of the Christian savior sometime in spring, not winter. Those sharp-eyed shepherds, you may recall, were tending their flocks when they noted the bright star blazing over Bethlehem. In the Middle East (as well as in Lamar, Colorado), you don't put sheep out to pasture until there's grass, and grass doesn't grow in the middle of winter.

But the concepts of renewal, rebirth, and salvation—core precepts for the Easter celebration—have roots that go even further and deeper in our human and spiritual history. In Greek mythology, the youthfully beautiful goddess Persephone was spirited away by the dark (and understandably cold and lonely) god of the underworld. After compulsory arbitration, involving Mount Olympus and parties with standing, a time-share was arranged. The goddess, it was determined, would spend half her time in the underworld, with her cold, dark husband, and half above, to share her warmth and beauty with the likes of us. The date of her reemergence was (of course!) the vernal equinox—and Persephone was just one of many spring goddesses worshiped by assorted ancient cultures, including Ashtoreth of the ancient Israelites, Ishtar of the Assyrians, and Cybele, the Phrygian goddess of fertility.

Actually, the story of Cybele cuts pretty close to the Christian bone. Cybele had a male consort, Attis, who, according to legend, was the product of a virgin birth and died, annually, only to be resurrected around the time of the spring equinox. The way to awaken the moribund deity was through song, dance, and merriment—i.e., a celebration.

And yes, certainly, the Christian Easter celebration has direct religious and historical ties to the Jewish festival of Passover. Few historians would deny it. And in the interest of balance, I am happy to point out that many fundamentalist Christians assert that any presumed earlier accounts having elements of or resemblance to the one, true Easter story are actually the work of Satan, who has engaged in a disinformation campaign to sow confusion and obfuscate the truth.

What do I think? I think that stories that vault ages do so not because they are or are not divinely inspired but because they resonate within the human soul. And that, ten thousand years from now, historians may be arguing about *Romeo and Juliet* and *West Side Story* and which came first.

Like the chicken and the egg. Like an empty tomb and a fulfilled promise.

Empty Vessels

The road was getting muddy, and when a trail opened to my right, my feet just took it. No plans, no conscious design. I just headed for the cliffs that defined the east side of the canyon where I had, as yet, not been.

They were composed of layer upon layer of ancient and compressed sand that once was the bottom of a sea. In this surface pocked by shallow grottoes and overhanging ledges, it would have been surprising not to find evidence of earlier visitors, and I wasn't disappointed. There were signs.

Christian names cut by the hands of people almost certainly in their graves. Petroglyphs of running bison, lances, and odd runic markings telling the story of some epic event that transpired long ago. The story and the storyteller were now resurrected in my mind, his bid for immortality as secure as my memory.

Best of all, and perhaps not unexpected, I found scores of cliff swallow nests clustered beneath the protective overhang. Some were old, broken vessels used many seasons ago. Others were fresh, intact, constructed last year or perhaps the year before. They hung like gourds or lanterns, their dark and empty openings resembling the open mouths of choral singers.

But the cliffs were silent, except for the hiss of snow. And the gourds, on this Easter Sunday, were empty. Devoid of life. Silent as tombs. As they had been since the birds had, last fall, fled south. Where, in some distant land, the birds had remained all winter.

And I smiled, because I knew that one hundred or two hundred or five hundred miles south, the builders of those nests were already en route to this place and these cliffs. That today, or tomorrow, or at the most a week from now, the cliffs would once again be filled with the frenetic comings and goings of swallows building and repairing nests and then filling them with life.

Empty vessels? Hardly. A person would have to be spiritually bankrupt to call something so filled with promise empty. And a person would have to be pretty dense not to see that, despite the snow, by the first weekend in April, spring was gaining on winter across the prairies of North America.

Old story. But none the worse for having been told, or celebrated, many ways and times before.

THE TRYSTING PLACE
I was right. The snow was gone by morning. Linda and I woke to a warm and beautiful spring day.

The primitive campground in Colorado's Two Buttes fish and game management area has two attributes that are irresistible to campers: scenic beauty and privacy. It is set in the cleft of a narrow sandstone canyon, mirrored in a small, clear lake. The water-sculpted red rock, the flanking cotton-woods flush with spring—everything about the place was a treat to the senses and a welcome change from the open landscape where Linda and I had spent so many weeks.

I don't know what it is about being in the open that makes people edgy. Maybe it's the wind. Maybe it's the scale. Maybe it's atavistic. We weak and defenseless primates just don't like being prey to a thousand watchful eyes in a place where we don't even have a decent tree to climb.

For whatever reason, the little canyon we'd sheltered in to avoid the storm was as welcome as it was welcoming.

"I'm going to find a way up to the top of that cliff," I announced shortly after breakfast.

"Okay," said Linda. Taking advantage of the light, she was composing photos of the seed-billowing cattails lining the water's edge. Photographers hate to waste good light.

Above the campsite, I crossed the earthen dam that served as the eastern rim of a nonexistent reservoir. Navigated a course to the cliff. Eased my fifty-six-year-old frame down to the projecting and wind-polished overlook that was the landform's most distinguishing feature, and discovered, quickly, and not surprisingly, that, once again, I was not the first to be so taken by the allure of Two Buttes.

Beneath my feet, cut into the 145-million-year-old rock,

were the names of individuals and couples who had preceded me. Clearly, my animal instincts had led me to the local trysting place.

Scenic beauty and a measure of privacy are key components of this human activity, too.

You may never have heard the term *trysting place*. It's old Scottish. It means "an appointed place of meeting." It also means "to fix, or agree upon," which sounds a lot like another word: *consent*.

Recognize the term or not, chances are that somewhere in your past (or present) you, and someone else, have known a trysting place. If you have not, I pity you. That night, or nights, you and another spent beneath the stars, feeling the cool embrace of stone, the cushioning caress of grass, and bodies and souls dissolving into one must rank among the greatest memories of the human experience.

Or possibly the worst. Maybe I was just lucky.

Across the lake, the cottonwoods were just coming into bloom. Red for male trees, lime green for females. So early in the season, only the topmost branches were in flower. Set against the sun-heated backdrop of the opposing cliffs, these subtle colors of spring's first blush seemed to kindle and glow. This was what I had originally climbed up here to see. Now it served as a backdrop to the stories cut in stone.

Feeling like a cross between an archaeologist and a voyeur, I studied the names, which offered testimony to epic transitions craving affirmation and recognition. If this wasn't the case, why commit your undying love to stone?

There were many names chiseled into the rocks, and many, on the outermost outcropping, were single and male, "stag," as we used to say back when I might have taken chisel to stone. The outcropping, I surmised, was a place for daredevils, a place of male passage. Make the leap into the lake below or be "chicken" (circa 1950) or "a wuss" (circa 1970) or . . . well, I wouldn't presume to know what someone is labeled today who will not commit himself to a forty-foot dive into Black Hole.

I only learned later that the place has a name and that it does indeed invite daredevils who sometimes break limbs and even lose their lives. A place of delicious ill omen, it is rumored to have cold, deep currents that sweep swimmers into underground chambers and is alleged to have swallowed a whole piece of earthmoving equipment "a long time ago."

The fascinating, but not surprising, thing is that, when I was in the age of passage, we had our own "black hole," known locally as the Brickyard Ponds, and the myths associated with the place were eerily similar. The Brickyard Ponds, too, were fed by treacherous underground springs that would knot the muscles of hapless swimmers, and there were rumored to be rusting hulks of earthmoving equipment in the depths, allegedly abandoned as the water flooded the pit after the cap on the subterranean spring was sprung.

Beer parties were a rite of passage on "the beach" of the Third Brickyard Pond. And, according to my source—a local

Lamar haircutter named Barbara (who hadn't been to the Black Hole in "oh . . . years")—few local high school students survived to responsible adulthood before being lured to Black Hole to down some brews, joust with fate, or . . .

A little farther back from the daredevil's ledge, on the smooth, polished, and sensually contoured stone, I found another reason to account for the place's popularity. Found the names of "Pete + Gracie," who committed their affection for each other to stone in 1991.

And not far away, big, bold letters attested to the bonding of "GARY" and "SANDY" along with a well-crafted heart and numbers expressed 19 & 81.

I guess this refers to the year 1981—ten years before Pete and Gracie and just about the time Ronald Reagan took office. The other possibility is that one of the pair was nineteen, and the other had been collecting Social Security for almost that many years (clearly the lesser of the two possibilities).

Not far away, in boxed and deep-cut letters I found: "I ♥ Ashley." No date. But clearly cut sometime after New York City inaugurated the now-ubiquitous I ♥ advertising campaign.

A plea to young lovers from future ero-ologists: Please remember to write the date. If your love's worth immortalizing, it's worth dating.

And remember to cut your letters as deep as your commitment. I note, sadly, that "NAME ABRADED AWAY" and "NAME ABRADED AWAY" encapsulated their love in a big, well-preserved heart back in 1951, but, alas, they are now, as a result of normal erosion, anonymous. All that hard rock cutting for nothing.

One inscription deserving special recognition states that "Susan ♥ Michael Night and Day." What makes this one special is not only the sentiment but the effort! It takes time to chisel into rock. This might explain why "Lupe n Germinia 9/23/06" barely scratched the surface with their boast and claim. Perhaps they were in a hurry. Perhaps their love wasn't meant to last. Some loves don't. And some of these failures must become committed to stone, too.

The very deeply cut notation "Scott Sucks" might fall into this category.

As I explored and studied, I began to see a pattern. Among those inscriptions bearing dates, the months May and September seemed most prevalent, seemed (by projection) to constitute the prime trysting seasons hereabouts. In part, this has to do with temperatures. Momentous days (and nights) must fall during times when the temperatures will support a measure of comfort and intimacy. And May is graduation time, a time of transition. I have noticed, in life, that major transitions are not regularly spaced. Often they come in a flurry.

September? I'm not sure. But it might fall at a point after harvest when there is time to "get away." And September is also the beginning of the school year. Again, a time of transition (and dyad shuffling, as a whole battery of hit music singles attests to).

One thing did seem clear. Most of the names cut in stone were of recent vintage—from the eighties, nineties, and this decade of the new century. I think that the softness of the stone has something to do with this. Sandstone is a very soft rock. Like love, it is affected by the forces of erosion. I think, too, that Two Buttes might not now have the popular recreational focus it once had. I'm basing this presumption only upon the waterless reservoir (flanked by boat launch ramps that end in dirt) and the fact that during the two days Linda and I camped here we encountered only one other camper, a vagabond horse packer looking for someplace to water and graze his animals.

Trysting places need, above all other things, a measure of privacy. You bring the ardor.

I don't know how many names are cut into the wind- and water-smoothed stone on the cliff above the pool. Five hundred is a safe bet. It might be a thousand. And after my search for names, I went in search of other artifacts that are part of the dowry of trysting places.

Beer cans, broken bottles, moldy blankets, blackened campfires, et cetera. I was surprised to find mercifully little. Discarded ankle socks seemed disproportionately represented (I found five), but all in all the place was remarkably tidy. The kind of place you wouldn't mind visiting yourself.

With a friend.

And as for that thing, that device, that key indicator of popular trysting places the world over—and don't even pretend to me that you don't know what I'm referring to; don't pretend to me that you are not the least bit curious—a surprise there, too.

Nope. Didn't find a one. Used or unused. Not even a wrapper. There's a lake below. And the cliff is a very windy place. And it was, after all, very early in the trysting season.

It might be that "safe sex" is little practiced here. I tend to doubt that. Or it might be that trysting here is very chaste, in league with the first blush of spring. I kind of doubt that, too.

Part of my skepticism has to do with basic human nature. Part of it has to do with memories that have lost little of the heat from the events that kindled them.

Part of it has to do with the prescient inscription I found on one of the cliff walls. Not cut in stone (the author didn't have time for this) but written in purple, epoxy-based ink. It read:

> Sex isn't the answer.
> Sex is the question.
> Yes is the answer.

And while I certainly don't question the accuracy of this, I will qualify it. In the time of first blush, the time of between, there is a much more alluring answer: "Maybe." *Maybe* is much closer to *want* than to *have,* and it's tenuous, like spring itself.

CHAPTER 6
Milnesand,
New Mexico

ON THE WINDWARD SIDE OF SPRING

On April 12, we crossed the Canadian River on Highway 385 beneath a sky dressed in beggars' rags and with grassland—tall, pale-on-to-translucent grass that rippled beneath the wind—stretching out on all sides. The "river" was a quarter-mile-wide sandbar, bracketed by ten-foot banks, with several sanctifying puddles in the middle. That's right. This corner of the prairies is exceedingly dry. Not quite desert. But dry enough. Most of the people who live here will be quick to tell you this. In fact, the burden of this curse is almost a point of pride among those tough enough to live on the dry rim of the agricultural edge. Farmers and ranchers are more mindful of rainfall totals than of the price of gas, and they mark on kitchen calendars and dog-eared journals the amount of every wet blessing down to the one hundredth of an inch.

The other thing they talk about is the wind.

"Cold front's coming through," I observed.

"Swainson's hawk!" Linda replied, trumping my observation with a discovery. Sure enough, pinned against the wind-whipped sky, rocking like a metronome with an inner ear disorder, was a Swainson's—the archetypal buteo of western grasslands. It was our first of the year. Something to celebrate.

The bird had spent the winter on the Pampas of Argentina with, perhaps, a million and a half kin. They were now returning to nest and rear the next generation. While there was no way of telling whether this individual was a local breeder or destined to make its way to the limits of the bird's breeding range, in Alaska, I was willing to bet it was home, here, on the Staked Plain of Texas and New Mexico. We'd entered the borders of this beautiful and frighteningly featureless terrain when we crossed the Canadian River.

Fifty thousand square miles of flatland and mantling sky—the largest level plain in the United States, stretching four degrees of latitude and longitude between the Canadian River to the north, the Edwards Plateau to the south, the Pecos River to the west, and the Red, Pease, Brazos, and Colorado rivers in the east. In terms of landmass, as artfully expressed in John Miller Morris's book, *El Llano Estacado* encompasses a region larger than the sum of the ten smallest thirteen original colonies. In terms of American history, the region bears the distinction of being the first part of the United States visited by Europeans, when Francisco Vásquez de Coronado set off with more than one thousand men on a quest for the fabled city of gold in 1540.

Coronado spent two years on his quest. And while the night encampments of fifteen hundred men and their horses are bound to leave an imprint upon the land, only two encampments have ever been found. The winds of the Staked Plains have erased almost all signs of their passage.

"Whoa," I said, as a gust of wind in the forty-knot range hit the Road Pig with a broadside, almost sending our modern-day prairie schooner into the oncoming lane.

Not that it mattered. There wasn't a car to be seen in either direction. But as we drew closer to the Texas Panhandle town of Hereford and headed on to Clovis, New Mexico, it began to matter a great deal. Both the wind and the traffic increased in scope and scale. Highway 60 cuts southwest, and the winds were dead on northwest, hitting us at a perfect right angle. All we knew or cared was that it was tough holding our high-profile vehicle on the road—and that it was getting increasingly difficult to see.

"Close your window!" Linda-ever-mindful-of-her-expensive-camera-equipment-Dunne shouted as our van penetrated a river of airborne dirt that had only yesterday belonged to the farmer whose newly plowed fields lay to the windward side of the road. The localized sandstorm was thick enough to make headlights more essential than prudent. It gave us a taste of what those settlers who endured the Dust Bowl era had experienced.

Literally. The flinty taste of wind-borne dust, infiltrating the van through nooks and crannies, settled on our tongues, parched our air passages, and, as the afternoon wore on, made our eyes feel as if they'd been worked over with emery cloth.

"Yep," one resigned resident observed without emphasis or exaggeration, "days like this we just sit here and watch Arizona passing by."

"Watch out!" Linda warned, with a great deal of emphasis (and only small exaggeration) as an empty cattle truck we were following began to writhe across both lanes of traffic.

"I'm watching," I said, which was getting increasingly harder to do.

Visibility as we approached Clovis went from intermittently poor to increasingly bad, and the winds that had been challenging before were approaching white-knuckle levels of concern. We learned, later, that wind gusts that afternoon at Cannon Air Force Base were measured in excess of sixty miles per hour. We were told, later, that dust storm reports and predictions were accepted elements of the daily newscast in parts of the Texas Panhandle. But at the RV park in Clovis, where we sought shelter fifty miles short of our destination, the winds seemed not to warrant much attention.

In response to my question regarding the wind and

what time the blow had started, the owner replied: "Hadn't noticed it come up."

And while I don't doubt the truth in this, the residents of the Llano Estacado are only too aware of air moving forcefully across their open landscape. When asked what it is that they most associate with spring, they don't say rain.

Rains, hereabouts, scant as they are, come mostly with the monsoonal flow of July and August.

They don't say "bursting buds" or "leaves on trees." Trees, in a land so featureless that Coronado was alleged to have planted stakes in order to navigate a straight course, are an anomaly.

In the Staked Plains, the Llano Estacado, they associate spring with wind. Lots of wind.

There is one possible exception to this. At the little crossroads community of Milnesand, New Mexico, spring means chickens. Prairie-chickens. These indicator species of the southern High Plains, and the hundred-odd registrants of the Sixth Annual High Plains Lesser Prairie-Chicken Festival who were descending upon Milnesand to view them, were why Linda and I were going there.

THE MILL IN THE SAND

The meteorological forces had called a truce when Linda and I set off next morning for Milnesand. Winds were moderate. Skies were western-sky blue, pocked by clouds that were western-movie-set perfect.

"Are you sure we're on the right road?" I asked.

"Why?" my navigator wanted to know.

"Well, because we just passed our second highway sign saying that we are so many miles from Tatum and no mention of anyplace called Milnesand in between.

"And," I added, "I don't know whether you've noticed it, but there doesn't seem to be a great deal of traffic on this road."

The truth of this observation, while patently obvious, was later certified by an independent study (conducted by me). On three occasions over the course of the next four days, I measured traffic volume on New Mexico Highway 206. In daylight hours, passing cars, northbound and southbound, averaged one car every two minutes. The survey site was, in fact, the crossroads hamlet of Milnesand. We found it. And you've heard the expression "don't blink or you'll miss it"? It very much applies to Milnesand. Milnesand is a contraction of the place's historic designation, "Mill in the Sand," the name given it by the cowboys of the old XIT ranch—in the late 1880s—at the time, the largest fenced cattle ranch in the world. Not far from the present location of the stone marker bearing the XIT brand is the Jody windmill. When the XIT was the law of the land, it represented the only reliable source of water in a near-desert landscape dominated by shin oak–covered dunes, deep sand, and a fragile coating of grass. And while the place might be phonetically known to the people in the Department of Transportation in Santa Fe (and Rand McNally) as "Mill-nuh-sand," many locals pridefully or stubbornly impart a historic inflection on the name. If you sit at the yellow tablecloth–covered table in the Kountry Kitchen General Store and Post Office, you'll hear residents—not that there are many of them—pronounce the name of the place "Mill-in-sand."

In fact, not counting the seasonal prairie-chicken technicians, who number about six, there are (as near as I can assess) precisely two people who might be said to live in the town. The post office, Zip Code 88125, serves sixteen post office box holders. The rural delivery route, servicing the outlying ranch community, takes four hours to cover, providing weather and road conditions are good. The "town" itself consists of the post office–store, a fire hall, a community center, a picnic area, one brick home, a Baptist church, several water towers, a few outbuildings, one gas pump, one public phone, and grazing land on all sides.

The gas pump bore a handwritten note: "Sorry. No gas." The phone, however, had a dial tone.

"Now I know why our contact told us to meet her at the post office," Linda observed, following a period of appraisal that lasted about as long as it took to take in the entire town, which was about as long as was necessary to slow down and park in the dirt lot that served the community center. "Where's the RV park?"

"I think we're in it," I said.

Yes, at first glance, and maybe second glance, too, the "Lesser Prairie-Chicken Capital of the World" seemed pretty short on human services. But that is precisely why the state and private lands around Milnesand have one of the largest and most viable lesser prairie-chicken populations on Earth. And what the place may lack in amenities, it more than makes up for in plain, honest hospitality.

"I'll bet that's her," I said as the door to the Kountry Kitchen opened and a lithe, quick-stepping woman emerged and immediately adopted a compass bearing that would intersect our van.

"Well," said Linda, "since she seems to be the only other person on the planet today, I'll bet you're right."

Tish McDaniels, manager of The Nature Conservancy's 18,500-acre Milnesand Preserve, is a slight, pixie-featured, middle-aged woman who has the energy and enthusiasm of a high school cheerleader and, beneath her open and friendly demeanor, the acumen of a career diplomat. Yes, her primary obligation is to the preserve and the fifteen hundred to two thousand lesser prairie-chickens that are on it. That is about one third of the New Mexico population.

But in order to accomplish this, she has found herself doing battle with oil and gas interests (who, it turns out, own the mineral rights to the sand beneath the preserve) and bringing her diplomatic skills to bear upon adjacent landowners, who have a deep-seated and not necessarily unwarranted distrust of outside people approaching them with strange agendas.

Tish is not an outsider; she is, in fact, the daughter of the former editor of one of Roosevelt County's most widely read newspapers. Or, as expressed to her by one of the local landowners, "Tish, we don't consider you one of Them."

While "Them" is a broad-based term covering anyone who was not born and raised on the Llano Estacado, in the context of prairie-chickens, "Them" constitutes New Mexico Department of Game and Fish people and "tree-huggers," as one local rancher expressed it (a curious label to apply on a treeless landscape—not that I pointed this out).

Homegrown or not, Tish is a dedicated conservationist. When she speaks about the land, the chickens, the research project, and conservation initiatives, she often uses possessive terms. When she gets particularly enthused about a topic, her hands move as quickly and demonstratively as chickens on a lek.

When not doing fieldwork herself, she is coordinating the surveys and research projects that are conducted by interns, attending conferences and meetings, soliciting grants, and doing much of the promotional and organizational work associated with the Prairie-Chicken Festival, which was, on the day of our arrival, two days away.

"Tish," I asked with no small measure of temerity, "do you have the time to show us a bit of the preserve?"

Of course she didn't. But an hour later, aboard Tish's Toyota Tacoma and astride the rutted tracks that stitch the preserve, she was speaking glowingly and knowingly about the native grasses of the mixed-grass prairies, expounding upon the importance of the shin oak community that is, to a large degree, the habitat that sustains New Mexico's prairie-chickens, and introducing us to some of the sixty-two active lesser prairie-chicken "booming grounds" (or leks) that are on TNC's property.

It was approaching noon. The leks were empty. No, not because the birds are rare. The U.S. Fish and Wildlife Service has determined that a designation of "threatened" is warranted, but official designation is pending. The leks were empty because displaying males knock off after midmorning. You want to see chickens, you got to get up early. And lots of people do want to see lesser prairie-chickens. Enough, at least, to hold a festival in their honor and to be forced to turn hopeful registrants away when the registration fills.

THE BEST LITTLE LESSER PRAIRIE-CHICKEN
FESTIVAL THIS SIDE OF THE CANADIAN, PECOS, RED,
PEASE, BRAZOS, AND RIO GRANDE RIVERS
The microphone emitted an electronic squeal of protest—which was quelled by the volunteer fire department chief and AV technician (who was standing by the control panel in the event of just such an emergency). Smiling shyly, a denim-clad and chicken festival-capped Willard Hicks welcomed one and all to the Sixth Annual High Plains Lesser Prairie-Chicken Festival and to Milnesand, the "Lesser Prairie-Chicken Capital of the World." While this boast is defensibly true, it does not in any way, shape, or form account for the hundred-odd registrants packed into the Milnesand Community Center, sopping up the last of their chili

with chunks of corn bread, or relishing their second and third homemade brownies. Some with nuts; some without. Milnesand is a real American community, and this means freedom of choice.

As Festival Emcee Hicks (who bears an uncanny likeness to Mr. Greenjeans of *Captain Kangaroo* fame) got on with his introductions and "housekeeping" duties, I used the time to mull the galvanizing magic of bird festivals in general and the very special qualities of this one.

I don't know how many of these festivals there are in North America, and my guess is that nobody does. Since their inception in the 1970s and '80s, they have proliferated like yeast in a brew vat and spread faster than a secret. Pitched to local chambers of commerce and departments of tourism as effective ways of bringing ecotourist dollars into a region, more than ten thousand bird-oriented festivals may exist by now. Open the pages of those publications that serve the birding community—*Bird Watcher's Digest, Birding, Birder's World, WildBird* magazines—and you'll find them crammed with invitations to various new and established festivals.

Most such festivals are struggling with attendance and the financial difficulties it brings. Most have not realized their expectations, and this is, to a large degree, because those expectations were poorly framed. Only a handful might be said to enjoy a broad national audience or be (dare I say it) financially solvent.

How, then, can you account for the success of a birding

festival held in a place where not only is there no chamber of commerce, but there is virtually no commerce? Even more confounding, how is it possible that for four of the six years of the festival, the organizers have had to turn people away and that this glut of popularity has been accomplished by no advertising whatsoever?

There are answers to these questions, and in sum they go a long way toward defining the elements that make a successful birding festival.

First, you must start with a real, desirable product—i.e., you've got to have something that serious birders really, really want and that casual birders (the "general public") can get jazzed about. You need a birding phenomenon.

It can involve great aggregations of a single species. Half a million cranes on the Platte. Several million migrating western sandpipers in Cordova, Alaska. Several hundred wintering bald eagles on the Connecticut River.

It can be a time and place where large numbers of different species can be viewed. Cape May, New Jersey, in the fall. McAllen, Texas, in the Rio Grande Valley, in the spring. Morro Bay, California, in winter.

Or it can be someplace where a very rare, very celebrated, and very desirable species can be viewed and enjoyed. Some bird like the lesser prairie-chicken; some place like Milnesand, New Mexico.

And while there is more than one prairie-chicken festival offered in North America, there is one thing that bird festivals must do to be successful. They must meet and exceed the expectations of attendees. Now, at the time of this writing, I know what the successful track record of the High Plains Lesser Prairie-Chicken Festival evidenced. This place really has chickens! This festival really delivers what it promises. Point-blank, in-your-face, watch-them-till-you-turn-to-stone looks at dozens (even scores!) of strutting, leaping, scrapping, foot-thumping, vocalizing, testosterone-supercharged prairie-chickens and . . .

At a bargain price. Upped, this year (after great debate) to a heart-stopping ninety dollars per person. Cash or check. Sorry, no credit cards.

What do you get for what amounts to a trip to a dental hygienist, dinner for two at a fair to middling restaurant, or a round of golf?

At Milnesand, you get Friday and Saturday din—— no, make that supper (this is ranch country). Chili and corn bread, barbecued brisket, baked potato, beans, salad, and dessert.

Breakfast on Saturday and Sunday. Make that second breakfast. Again, this is ranch country. You get coffee and doughnuts prior to heading out to the leks before sunrise. Eggs, bacon and sausage, and pancakes (and all the leftover doughnuts you can eat) are served after the vans full of chicken viewers return.

Saturday lunch (grass-fed beef burgers on the grill). Transportation to and from prairie-chicken leks. Field trips devoted to prairie restoration, playa lakes, archaeology, and prairie dog biology.

Plus some very special regional entertainment that may or may not be unique but does place the High Plains Festival in a very exclusive class. On Saturday afternoon, attendees were treated to the parade ground maneuvers of a group of local ladies on horseback known as "The Cow Belles." Dressed like the Fourth of July. Topped off with white hats. Bracketed by both the American and state of New Mexico flags, the Belles galloped, wheeled, and maneuvered in semi-synchronous fashion to the accompaniment of a carefully selected, prerecorded set of country and western songs and the applause of attendees.

On Saturday night, the handlebar-mustached cowboy poet Charles Dixon, Ph.D., entertained listeners with a selection of verses spun on the lone prairie whose subjects ranged from a cowboy's love for his horse (two poems), his love for his wife (one poem), and other important developments falling between birth, death, and the recycling of a dead cowpoke's sub-spiritual matter.

Now that I think about it, this poem had something to do with horses, too. Something alimentary.

He didn't leave out a single authentic snort, choke, cough, or throat-clearing rattle. He was genuinely (and infectiously) teary-eyed at the mention of his wife. She was sobbing.

Included, but not touted, in the cost of admission was the opportunity to meet and talk chickens with many of the local ranchers and landowners, because one of the very special charms of the High Plains Festival is this local, homespun element. These are real ranches. This is a real ranch community. The meals are organized by the local women (and the proceeds benefit the community center and fire station). Any money left over after the bills are paid goes to the community, too.

It doesn't get more real than this. Places where members of the ranching community and the birding community can sit down and break bread are sadly few and far between. Which brings us to another key ingredient of a successful birding festival, right up there with good birds, good food, and a good agenda.

This is audience. For a bird festival to succeed, it must be able to draw from some (usually nearby) population centers. Most of those in the audience hailed from Albuquerque and Santa Fe. Only a handful were from out of state (including a contingent of six from Sun City, Arizona).

Linda and I won the "door prize" for "farthest distance traveled."

This is actually where most start-up birding festivals go awry, set themselves up for failure. Organizers approach the challenge believing and pursuing the notion that they will be attracting people from all over North America, who will come to the area and support local commerce. They spend their promotional dollars competing, with all those other festivals, for people from distant parts, overlooking the fact that their greatest participant base lies within half a day's drive.

Hint to organizers: You want a successful birding festival? Think globally, promote locally.

And this brings up the final key ingredient, which is organizers—and I don't necessarily mean "organizations in-volved." Most birding festivals do have a hosting organiza-tion or organizations that share the myriad tasks and duties inherent in bringing lots of people together in the same place at the same time. The organizations sponsoring the High Plains Festival include The Nature Conservancy, the Grasslans Foundation, and New Mexico Game and Fish. All work in concert; each shoulders its share of the work.

But in every human endeavor, including, and maybe particularly, endeavors that involve a number of individuals and interests, there is almost always one (or two or at most three) people who provide the power and the drive, who just plain keep the train on the track. In the case of the High Plains Festival, we're talking about a two-piston engine in the form of Tish McDaniels and Willard Hicks.

Other people contribute. Other people are entitled to their bows. But when the chips are down, when . . .

More vans have to be rented at the last minute, the toilet in the community center's ladies' room gets cranky, a snow-storm pins registrants down in Albuquerque, and some guy from New Jersey wants to know whether it would be too much trouble to . . .

It comes down to the event organizers. And as I was completing my musings, Emcee Hicks was finishing up his housekeeping chores. Introducing the ladies in the kitchen (who enjoyed their well-deserved applause). Thanking the many communities and organizations who provided vans and printed posters, supplies, and handout materials. The field trip leaders, whose freely given knowledge is beyond price. And, last but not least, introducing the evening's speaker:

"Tish McDaniels. Who will give us an overview of prairie-chicken biology."

Surprised? You shouldn't be.

A CHICKEN RUNS THROUGH IT

The microphone was passed. The PowerPoint projector turned on. And Tish McDaniels launched herself into her favorite subject. A discussion of the bird, its needs, its challenges, and its appeal.

So what is it about this bird that inspires people to plop down a ninety-dollar registration fee, commit a weekend in spring, get up at hours that would challenge a rural paper route delivery person, and journey to a town so tiny that they don't even drop the posted highway speed of sixty-five miles per hour for drivers passing through?

Lesser prairie-chicken is a highly specialized grouse that not only thrives in the dry, midgrass prairies of the High Plains, but is restricted to it.

The problem with specialization is that your greatest strength, your ability to thrive in a limiting condition, is also your greatest strategic weakness. You live by a habitat, you die by it, too. Where once the booming sound of this bird on its spring lek was second only to the sound of the wind as a mechanism for inducing human madness, now the sound of booming males, the sound of spring perking on the prairies, occurs on only 8 percent of the bird's historic range—a range that has been reduced largely by the conversion of the prairies to agricultural land.

This may be the single largest challenge to the lesser prairie-chicken, but it is not the only one. Much of the remaining grouse habitat is on private land or open range, where birds must compete with cattle in an industry with a notoriously low profit margin. The temptation for landowners to overgraze their land is immense.

In addition, this is a species that is adapted to live in a habitat without trees or other vertical structures—the kind that offer hunting birds of prey a strategic edge. Our species likes to plant trees. Our species likes to erect wind turbines and put in oil and gas fields, and these must be serviced by roads that cut through the native vegetation, fragmenting tracts of land and opening the front (and back and side) door to a host of grouse-eating predators.

Fire suppression, in a fire-based ecosystem, has also had an impact, allowing invasive or grouse-unfriendly vegetation to flourish at the expense of native and beneficial plant species. Herbicides, depending on how and why they are applied, may do the same thing. Locally, the dominant vegetative cover of shin oak (literally, an oak that gets as high as your shins) is very important to grouse as a source of both food and cover. But it competes with native grasses for space and water, and its buds are toxic to cattle, so it is actively, and sometimes ruthlessly, controlled by ranchers.

Speaking of control, even the decades-long (and very

successful) campaign to eliminate prairie dogs may have had a deleterious effect on prairie-chickens. Prairie dog towns, with their close-cropped vegetation, constituted perfect booming ground habitat for prairie-chickens. The perfect place to be seen, the perfect place to see approaching danger. Also, prairie-chickens benefit from the rich and diversified array of food plants that prairie dog disturbance spawns.

It's an old story. You push an environment here, something unforeseen falls off the edge over there. And while many ranchers would love to see prairie dogs disappear from the landscape, very few would want to see prairie-chickens join them.

In a similar vein, not all of the habitat alterations perpetrated upon the prairies by our species have been harmful. On the Milnesand Preserve, many (and perhaps most) of the chicken leks are found on the devegetated sites of old, capped oil wells or the trampled ground around cattle water tanks. In the fall, particularly, hundreds of grouse may gather on milo fields, drawn to the surfeit of unharvested waste grain.

And the fact remains that many, and perhaps most, of the lesser prairie-chickens alive today are found on private ranchland. It isn't right, correct, or fair to blame ranchers for the bird's decline.

One thing that is uncontested and absolutely clear is that grouse populations themselves are subject to periodic and dramatic swings, and these may be related to periods of drought. Every twenty to thirty years, the populations crash, with the most recent decline having occurred in the late 1980s and early '90s. But as accepted and anticipated as these fluctuations might be, they do not mask or address a profound and undermining fact. When prairie-chicken populations recover, they never reach the numbers present before the crash. Year by year, cycle by cycle, the North American population of lesser prairie-chickens declines. That's the bad news.

But just like supply and demand in economics, the less you have of something, the more valuable or esteemed it becomes. If you are lucky enough to be sitting atop one of the last viable populations of lesser prairie-chickens within their very limited range (or, if you prefer, "the world"), then you've got something of value. Something worth promoting. Something worth selling.

This might not be the only, or even the primary, reason people flock to see prairie-chickens. Or why a mom-and-pop festival in the Middle of Nowhere, New Mexico, is so successful.

But it sure doesn't hurt.

REVEALED AT LAST:
WHY THE CHICKEN CROSSED THE ROAD
Our fifteen-passenger van bumped its way along in the predawn darkness, turned, stopped. The driver, a young, sparsely mustached conservation officer with New Mexico Game and Fish, asked whether anyone among the six fe-

male and three male chicken watchers wanted to exchange seats for a better view.

Have you ever birded from the confines of a fifteen-passenger van? It is one of the most universally used and universally hated automotive institutions in the bird-watching industry. If you have not, and if you have never considered birding a contact sport, it can mean only that you have never seen five birders all scrambling to get into the same front seat at the same time (while the original occupant is still in it).

One of the van's occupants dubbed the exercise "Chicken Twister."

After order was restored, and the two conservation officers settled in to make themselves inconspicuous, we nine chicken aspirants got down to the serious business of listening intently and willing on the dawn—prime time for lesser prairie-chickens.

It was a beauty. Without question one of the finest sunrises I've ever experienced (and I've seen thousands). A classic ROY G BIV morning, with a crescent moon–stamped and star-studded sky over a black-on-black earth becoming knit by a rainbow-colored seam: red, orange, yellow, green, blue, indigo, violet.

"I hear one," the woman who'd won first place in the seat competition proclaimed.

More than one, actually. The spectral touch of morning sunlight had brought the prairies to percolate. In short order, the sound of "gobbling" lesser prairie-chicken males reverberated around the lek and spilled over into the van and the ears of its occupants.

I don't know why they call it "gobbling." The label is no more descriptive or accurate than the other often applied description, "booming." But all efforts to describe the sound of a bunch of hormonally fueled male prairie-chickens are doomed to failure, complicated as the phenomenon is not only by multiple birds but by an array of vocalizations. There are clucks. There are descending chortles that sound like a cross between a chicken's cackle and a kookaburra's laugh. There are peevish whines. There are rippling burbles that sound like a coffee percolator throwing a tantrum or sheet metal rippling in the wind. And remember, there are multiple birds! Commonly, all these sounds are heard at once, and the conjoined cacophony sounds like a cross between a crowded hen house and a penny arcade, sounds like spring coming to a boil.

It is, in short, amazing. Once it reverberated across the High Plains, with leks scattered a mile apart. Today, it is a privilege and a thrill to hear it at all.

Long before the suggestions of birds became the shadows of birds became the forms of birds, the sound of prairie-chickens on the lek was the focus of all within the van.

Except for one of the conservation officers, who used the opportunity to catch up on his sleep.

Just as with the cranes on the Platte River, it is this element of sound that seems to make the experience of viewing chickens at the lek special, but with one very important difference. While the sound of cranes coming in to roost is moving unto profound, the sound of a bunch of male prairie-chickens on the lek just plain makes you want to giggle.

And when it's finally light enough to see the birds strutting their stuff, it's all you can do to keep from laughing out loud. In fact, some people, most notably all the women in our group, seemed unable to resist. At times the sound of their giggles rivaled the sound of the birds.

The lek was about the size of a gym floor, but most of the males, fourteen in number, were displaying within fifty feet of the van. Some were less than ten feet away. By luck or design, we'd parked right across from the center of the lek. The birds were all but oblivious to our presence.

A lek is part square-dance floor, part gladiatorial arena, with a touch of May Day festivity thrown in. Scattered across the open plain were individual birds, each defending a hard-won territory. His trysting space. The place he defends from rival males and the place roving females may visit. Providing, of course, the resident male has the "right stuff."

The birds in the center of the lek have the best sites, and since these are the best sites, it necessarily follows that the birds in the center are the biggest, baddest, toughest, scrappiest birds.

The chickens with the "right stuff."

Chickens with the right stuff strut it to females by leaning forward, puffing themselves up, erecting their pinnae into hornlike projections, inflating their bright yellow eye combs and raspberry-colored esophageal air sacs, thumping their feet in a mincing jig, turning, and throwing themselves aloft.

In between dance sets, they vocalize. Their bodies, convulsing at every note, make the birds look like they are trying to cough up pellets.

G-lulp. 'lulp. 'lulp. 'lulp-lulp-lulp-lulp . . .

It looks ridiculous. It is ridiculous. Small wonder the women in the group were giggling.

Some of the giggles were short, muffled. "Huh," or "hum." These were most common, often expressed in conjunction with hands brought to mouths.

Other giggles were more emphatically two-noted. "H-huh." Commonly executed with terse backward tosses of the head.

Occasionally, giggles were louder and more protracted (and usually given in response to a male chicken doing something really testosterone fueled—such as charging a distracted rival and knocking him on his vent).

"Huh-h-h-h-hm." These full giggles often elicited responses from the other female chicken watchers, resulting in a giggling chorus.

By and large (and except for the conservation officer who was snoring softly), males in the van remained silent—either respectfully so or embarrassedly so. The fact is, the female-attracting antics of male chickens on the lek strike too close to home.

But let's put interspecific courtship stuff into perspective.

In the history of the world, no male prairie-chicken has ever gone up to a female prairie-chicken and said: "Can I buy you a drink?" No male prairie-chicken has ever spent an afternoon washing and waxing his car for Friday night. No prairie-chicken has ever spent so much as one sweaty minute in a fitness center. No prairie-chicken has ever taken a performance-enhancing drug (unless shin oak buds have some undiscovered arousal properties, in which case The Nature Conservancy stands to reap a fortune).

And in the interest of equality, it should also be pointed out that no female prairie-chicken has ever split a seam trying to get a size-eight butt into size-six jeans. No prairie-chicken has ever pierced body parts, had a nose job or breast implants, engaged the services of an online dating service, gone on a blind date, or even changed the color of her plumage.

Frankly, when you consider some of the things human males (and females) do to gain the attention of suitors, puffing yourself up, dancing, and exposing secondary sex organs doesn't seem very silly at all. Come to think of it, don't we do all those things, too?

Comical aspects aside, the spectators in the van were transfixed by the pageantry and motion. It seemed choreographed. It seemed almost orderly. It was about that time that the first hen arrived, and the birds with the right stuff got right into one another's faces.

Stepping away from the grass on the far side of the road, poised as an Oscar nominee stepping out of the limo and onto the red carpet, was a prospecting female. She crossed the road, slowly but directly, and settled right into the territory of a very well positioned male (a veritable Baryshnikov among chickens, with perhaps a touch of Sylvester Stallone). The favored male took this show of approval very personally. In fact, he pretty much worked himself into a strutting, foot-stomping, quivering fit. So did the birds on four adjacent leks, who alternately did their best to catch her eye and distract his. The way they did this was by crowding Mr. Right's territory.

The lines between chicken territories are etched in the minds of rival birds, not in the sand, and they have been drawn and redrawn by a thousand border clashes. The bird whose territory lay just to the north of our lady's champion pushed the limit, forcing Mr. Right to excuse himself from his visitor and deal with the border threat.

The rival birds crouched, like sumo wrestlers in the rink, like they'd already done a thousand times before. Sometimes males clash, in a flurry of feathers and striking feet. This time they did not. It was just a test, a show of force. The rival challenged. Mr. Right addressed it, calling the other bird's bluff, making sure that his flank was, at least for now, secure. He, after all, had things to do.

So, it turned out, did she. Another, smaller female arrived. Multiplying the commotion on the lek, distracting the alpha male, and prompting the first female to escort the new arrival to a place of relative inactivity. She did this by chasing her.

Then, perhaps to chide her diffident champion, the

alpha female positioned herself smack in the middle of the junction of five male territories—no man's land. Then, surrounded by five amorous suitors, not one of which dared breach lek protocol by crossing the line, she calmly crouched and made a great show of nibbling at the tips of forbs she didn't want.

For the next hour, she vacillated between this provocative sanctuary and the home ground of her primary suitor. He divided his attention between winning her back and beating back repeated challenges from the male to his right—Mr. Almost Has the Right Stuff.

The attention of the other attending males never wavered, and neither, I might add, did ours. Unspoken, but on everyone's mind, was a single question. Will she or won't she? Or, as framed by the napping conservation officer, who stirred himself long enough to express the male point of view:

"Is she still [*!*] teasing that poor guy?" The missing word was implicit, not spoken, but universally understood.

When it finally happened, if you blinked you missed it. She crouched. He mounted.

"Finally," three of the women in the van breathed, in chorus.

But at this moment of supreme triumph (just when Mr. Right was most vulnerable), the Evil Chicken from the North broke all established treaties, charged across the other bird's territory, and sucker-punched Mr. Right from behind, sending him flying.

It really was a low blow; by any standards of male conduct, fowl play. Witnessing it, you began to understand something of the depths of the bad feeling between the two birds.

But was the copulation successful?

Seemed it was. Even uncontested, chicken love is fast, lasting hardly more than a second or two. She stood and shuddered (like you may have seen post-copulating hens do in the barnyard). He didn't attempt to mount her a second time. In fact, the chosen bird seemed much more intent upon seeking retribution.

In something under a minute, the apparently satisfied female took wing, crossing back over the road. Puzzlingly, the other female (who now had the boys all to herself) went with her.

Maybe some chickens just like to watch.

Another minute later, a minute during which all the male birds more or less did nothing, the remaining birds took off, flying in various directions. Their work here was done.

After another brief bout of Chicken Twister, our van edged back onto the road and toward a 9:00 rendezvous with pancakes and bacon at the community center. It was only 7:30 A.M. The entire affair had taken less than two hours.

So there you are. Now you know. The next time someone asks you why the chicken crossed the road, you'll have the answer. Chances are you knew it all along.

CHAPTER 7

Comanche Grassland, Colorado

THE PRAIRIES GET A NEW DEAL

In 1935 the southern High Plains were in the fourth and fifth year of drought, the sixth year of an economic depression, and the middle of one of the greatest man-made ecological disasters in human history. Before it was over, the drought stripped the soil from as many as 100 million acres of prairie.

Plowed under by homesteaders and absentee farmers. Left fallow when grain markets collapsed. Baked and pulverized under a merciless sun. There was nothing to stop the prairie winds from lifting the soil from the earth and throwing it back into the faces of "nesters." The fallout from these prairie dust storms, or "dusters," ultimately reached Washington, D.C.—literally and figuratively.

There is a famous story about Hugh Hammond Ben-

nett, a soil conservation maverick and the soon-to-be director of a newly minted agency within the Interior Department, who in 1935 was embroiled in a do-or-die effort to secure congressional funds for land restoration. As much
showman as visionary, he asked for a twenty-four-hour
delay on the scheduled hearing after learning from contacts
in the weather service that the fallout from the now infa-
mous Black Sunday dust storm was tracking east and was
due to hit Washington, D.C., the following day.

For once, the weather service got it right. While Bennett
was at the podium. And as the sky turned the color of cop-
per and an eerie, dusklike darkness settled over and into the
Senate office building, Bennett shouted, "This, gentlemen,
is what I'm talking about. There goes Oklahoma."

His point demonstrably made, money was found for a
Soil Conservation Service, and at the same time a new New
Deal agency, the Resettlement Administration, was created
and given authority to buy back, from willing sellers, the
"submarginal" land that the government had been virtually
giving away to homesteaders since 1860. A buyout!

In 1937 the somewhat hastily conceived Resettlement
Administration morphed into the Farm Security Administration, and it is largely because of the efforts of these two
agencies that some 11.3 million acres of degraded lands
were purchased by the federal government between 1933
and 1946, when the buyback program was halted.

In 1953 these New Deal–spawned acquisitions were
transferred to the U.S. Forest Service, which in turn trans-

ferred much of the land to other state and federal land management agencies, including the Bureau of Land Management and the Fish and Wildlife Service.

Left in Forest Service hands were 3.8 million acres, which in 1960 were designated nineteen "national grasslands" to be managed for multiple uses, including outdoor recreation, range, minerals, and wildlife (and, of course, you). A twentieth grassland, Butte Valley National Grassland, in Northern California, was dedicated in 1991.

The Dust Bowl was an ecological disaster on an almost unimaginable scale. The recovery has been slow. The lesson painful. But if there is one good thing to have risen from the disaster, it is this: without it, there would be no national grasslands. One of them is the Comanche Grassland of Colorado.

Your Man on the Comanche

A jacketed Linda and short-sleeved district ranger Tom Peters started walking back across the four-week-old burn, their enthusiasm finally eroded by the sustained thirty-five-mile-per-hour winds (and thoughts of lunch). But I lingered, looking at the fire-blackened mound rising ever so slightly above the prairie landscape and its complement of charcoal-grilled yuccas with new awareness and a visceral excitement.

"I get it," I said to the toasted tips of plants that more nearly resembled charred artichokes than the spiky clusters of untouched yuccas lying outside the prescribed-burn area.

"I get it," I said again, this time to the Cassin's sparrow, keyed up on a yucca that had, by some incalculable combination of small forces (like wind speed and direction, topography, ground moisture, surrounding vegetation), completely escaped the flames.

Four weeks ago, when the 640-acre section had been torched by U.S. Forest Service personnel in a "prescribed burn," I might not have "gotten it." Understood it, yes.

"Fire is an important management tool for the maintenance of . . . and yada yady yah."

"Grasslands are fire-adapted ecosystems, and unless subjected to periodic . . . BLAH blah BLAH, blah, blah."

But not *gotten* it. In my gut. Where true empathetic understanding lies. I might well have looked on the smoldering landscape and seen it as charred waste, seen it . . .

Through Smokey Bear eyes. The view I was given as a kid—in books and stories and television informercials and half a thousand posters hung in every park or natural area I ever visited—showing a somber, shovel-bearing, dungaree-clad bruin with a bunch of furry fire victims standing all around him, their anthropomorphized heartbreak underscored by the dire warning:

Only you (always underscored!) can prevent forest fires.

The U.S. Forest Service got a lot of promotional mileage out of that bear. I (and every other responsible camper) broke my matches in two and doused my campfires with water until they were "dead out." Fire-deprived forests responded by building up a stockpile of combustible fuel that exploded, most spectacularly, in the Yellowstone Park fires of 1988, setting off a firestorm of debate in the halls of Congress.

What a delicious irony that it took a Forest Service district ranger and a grassland to show me the catalytic importance of fire.

Tom Peters is a tall, trim, fifty-four-year-old career forest ranger–the job every Smokey Bear-loving kid growing up in suburbia dreamed of (even if only briefly). Tom, a military brat, grew up outside Oakland, California, and went on to graduate from Humboldt State College with a degree in wildlife biology, making a life with the Forest Service a reality.

"I did all the wrong things for all the wrong reasons but still ended up with a great career," he said, with a practiced polish that served only to underscore, not obfuscate, the lie. An intelligent, organized, clear-thinking, and dedicated civil servant, he wears a confidence that is real, not assumed. He takes his administrative duties seriously and admits that the challenges of his job, which involve balancing the conflicting interests of multiple constituents and the ecological needs of the land under his care, sometimes makes sleep elusive.

The Forest Service, like the Bureau of Land Management, practices a policy of "multiple use" and "sustained yield."

Multiple use means hiking, hunting, bird watching, camping, gas and oil drilling, timber harvesting, and cattle grazing. *Sustained yield* means you can do what you want to do as long as the ecological integrity of the habitat is not diminished or destroyed.

But with an early retirement option a year away, and no plans to take it, it is plain that the man riding herd on the Comanche National Grassland accepts his obligations because he loves his workplace—443,000 acres of your grasslands—and because, by and large, he enjoys a good relationship with his boss.

Which is you. The people who own North America's public lands. It also includes Linda and me, and when we asked the district ranger for an hour or two to explain the importance of national grasslands, he converted it into a reason to get out of his office and into his workplace.

We climbed into a white Chevy four-by-four bearing U.S. Government plates. We turned left, and we were driving through your other backyard—the one you own but have probably never seen. The one Tom and fewer than one thousand Forest Service employees maintain for you.

Actually, there are about thirty-five thousand Forest Service personnel who manage and maintain 190 million acres of Forest Service land. But fewer than one thousand are assigned to the nation's twenty national grasslands, whose total acreage comes to about 4 million acres.

That you've never seen. Even though you've probably driven right through it!

"Where do you want to go?" Tom asked. "I got the feeling

last time we spoke that you didn't necessarily want to go to any of the canyons."

"We're mostly interested in prairies," I agreed. "And seeing them through your eyes."

If I'm not mistaken, my answer made him smile.

WHY?

Americans are freedom-loving people, and while freedom can be defined in many ways, the way most Americans think of freedom is freedom of movement—the latitude to go where you want to go, when you want to go there. This, and the fact that we have lots of places to go and lots of places to see, is why so many Americans take to the road each year to visit the great and scenic natural wonders of the country. I suspect you are one of them.

If you open the *Rand McNally Road Atlas* (which you probably keep in your car or in your home office) and turn to the map of the United States (bracketing pages 2 and 3), you'll find some of those celebrated destinations highlighted in eye-catching green. Places such as Mount Rainier, Yellowstone, Grand Teton, Rocky Mountain, and Grand Canyon national parks.

Chances are you have traveled on interstates en route to these destination hot spots. If so, and if you were driving on I-94 on the way to, say, Glacier National Park or the Little Bighorn Battlefield, then you passed right through the Little Missouri National Grassland as you exited North Dakota. It's not because you blinked. This designated national grassland covers 1,028,051 acres. If you were on your way to Yellowstone National Park on I-90, you were right on the nation's grassland mainline driving through Buffalo Gap and Thunder Basin national grasslands, and passing within sight of Fort Pierre National Grassland as you navigated the stretch between exits 226 and 221.

If you ever headed west on I-80, toward Cheyenne, Wyoming, or tacked south on I-76 en route to Rocky Mountain National Park, you were within a short drive of the Pawnee National Grassland (the interstates bracket the two sections). And if you were on I-40, heading, perhaps, for Death Valley, you passed very close to the Black Kettle National Grassland as you exited Oklahoma and entered the Texas Panhandle but were an hour or two south of the Rita Blanca and Kiowa national grasslands of Texas and New Mexico, respectively. The Kiowa grassland and the Comanche grassland of Colorado are closer to and better served by I-25.

So there you are. There you have it. If you've ever done the all-American cross-country drive (on your teenage lark . . . with the preteen kids . . . as your gift-to-me retirement present), you drove right past some of North America's most spacious, spectacular, and welcoming natural areas.

Your grasslands. You own them. What could be more welcoming than that?

So why didn't you stop?

I posed the question to Tom as we pulled off a county-maintained road and onto a rutted tract.

"No trees, no big mountains," he said with a shrug, and perfect candor. "What everybody tells you is that 'there's nothing between the Mississippi and the Rockies.'"

By the way, Linda and I have done the all-American drive-across-the-country thing eight or ten times. We drove right by most of those neat grasslands, too.

But not today.

We turned off the road. Opened a gate. Drove out on a two-tire track. Pulled up in an area bisected by barbed wire fences. That Tom said had been burned.

Really?

In between exclamations of "this is coming back great!" and "look at the growth on this western wheatgrass!" Tom explained some of the management principles at play on this particular allotment. How "that section over there" had been heavily grazed, and "this one had not." The lands had been swapped. Both had been burned. The difference between the way the two sections were coming back was apparent. Apparent, at least, to Tom.

I was still trying to find evidence that the habitat had recently burned at all. The only difference I could see was that the area that was heavily grazed was studded with fire-yellowed prickly pear cactus. The ungrazed area was mostly cactus-free.

But in the weeks since the burn, spring had worked its magic. All I could see was regenerating grass and a bounty of prairie flowers.

But stimulating growth and maintaining prairies is precisely what fires do. I might not have been able to see signs of the burn; I couldn't help but see the results.

Accepting the essential goodness of fire is not an easy conversion for most people (and not a few cattlemen, seeing nothing but their cattle's weight gain going up in smoke, don't accept it at all). But in essence, prairie is prairie because it isn't wet enough to be a forest. Trees require more water than grass. Where rainfall amounts are insufficient to maintain forests, you get prairies.

But the line between wet enough and not is not absolute. Rainfall totals differ year to year and, in fact, years to years. Weather patterns come in cycles. A series of wet years, when rainfall is generous (annual totals amounting to fifteen, twenty, even thirty inches of rain), will be followed by a series of dry years, during which annual rainfall may not exceed (in fact may fall well below) ten inches.

Some tree species require relatively little water, but even the most drought-resistant trees are hard-pressed to survive multiple years of near-desert-defining rainfall levels. It is probably more accurate to say that periodic drought, more than average rainfall, is the factor that determines where forest ends and prairie begins, but the line cannot be sharply drawn here, either.

The eastern tallgrass prairies, it turns out, receive enough rainfall for trees to flourish—yet until pioneer settlement they remained grasslands. In addition, there are some woody plants—such as sand sage and shin oak—that are very drought tolerant and, if left unchecked, will flourish at the expense of grasses.

There is, then, another ecological determinant working to keep prairie prairie, and that element is fire. If climate creates prairies, fire is the partner that helps maintain it. Grass not only is more tolerant of fire than most tree species but is, in large part, dependent upon it.

It works like this. When you look at grass, you are really seeing only a fraction of the plant. Somewhere between 60 and 80 percent of grass resides underground. This network of roots may reach over ten feet in some taller prairie grasses (and even the root system of the short-stemmed blue grama, a mixed prairie grass species, may extend six feet down). Prairie fires can burn hot, but they also burn quickly. Flames may shoot up over ten feet, but flames don't burn down, so where the prairie surface may be singed, the earth just below the surface is untouched and the roots, the essential core of the plant, are unaffected.

Grasses have another specialized adaptation that allows them to excel in a fire-rich environment. The growth point of grass is at the base, extending slightly above but mostly below the surface. Have you ever pulled a blade of grass and bitten into the soft, sweet, succulent base? That's the growth point—and its subterranean nature makes it fire resistant. Trees are different. The growth points on trees are at the tips of the twigs—fully exposed, fully vulnerable.

Prairie fires flash over grass and make toast out of the growing points of trees.

Grass is not just a passive beneficiary of fire. It both promotes fire and profits from it. The fuel for prairie fire is grass. While estimates differ, most experts believe that fires (either natural or spawned by Native Americans) flashed over native prairies every three to ten (some say thirty) years. The longer the interval, the more opportunity woody plants have to take hold. But delay only adds fuel, meaning accumulated litter, to the fire. More fuel means a hotter fire, so even established young tree saplings have more heat to beat when fire has its day.

Fire's parting gift to grass is the nutrient recharge that occurs in the wake of the flames. Plants get their energy from the sun but their nutrients from the soil. Like the phoenix of lore, grass, when it is ashed, releases key minerals to be taken back into the soil and then taken up again by new growth. Thus fertilized, grasses grow faster and stronger, and those other plants associated with the prairie ecosystem (like spring flowers!) come up more quickly, too.

"Any particular reason why this area was burned?" I asked Tom, as we headed back to the SUV.

"To create habitat for mountain plover," he explained. Mountain plover, a prairie obligate and a species of special concern.

"Seen any plover?" I asked.

"Nope," he said. "And between you and me, I think that long-billed curlew is a better prairie indicator."

"Seen any curlews?"

"Lots," he said. "Banner year."

Pretty soon, we were seeing them, too.

Lots.

LEARNING TO SEE

For curiosity's sake, we headed on over to a nearby allotment. This is the place where one of the most recent tornadoes was supposed to have touched down. We thought we might be able to find the twister's track.

I used the opportunity to ask Tom about the challenges of his job. As I might have expected (and you might have expected, too), managing grasslands is easy. The challenge is managing people.

"Finding and keeping good people" was the first issue and his greatest challenge, Tom expressed. The nation's grasslands are mostly located in remote areas—far from the coddling environment of suburbia. You find them near (and sometimes not so near) isolated and somewhat amenity-deprived rural communities.

The simple lifestyle is not for everyone, and this ambivalence is not limited to Forest Service personnel. The population on America's prairies has been declining for eighty years. In many places it is down to fewer than six people per square mile—the official designation for the frontier. In Baca County, the population density is approaching one person per square mile. That's the Census Bureau's designation for "wilderness." Ambitious young people who leave rural communities to attend college commonly do not return. They go where the job opportunities are, and they quickly become accustomed to the social amenities they find in college towns.

The second challenge was "the budget"—every administrator's bugaboo. But while I assumed that at issue would be "amount," the problem Tom focused upon was the short-term nature of the process. Budgets, in the federal system, are submitted and passed annually. The problem is that in wildlife management, experimental and restoration initiatives don't commonly fit a one-year timetable. Often, for results to be shown or proven, projects require multiple years. It's difficult putting projects into play when continued funding is always in question.

The third problem Tom mentioned was the multijurisdictional nature of his fief. The national grasslands are not, for the most part, intact. When the grasslands were instituted, farmland parcels were acquired from willing sellers—a seller here, a seller there. There was no overall design, no coercion exerted to get landowners to sell if they were reluctant.

The result was a fragmented mosaic of lands—some publicly owned, some privately. The right thing, the sensible thing from both an ecological and a management standpoint, would be to approach grasslands management by focusing on the entire ecosystem. But the Forest Service cannot conduct a controlled burn, or limit cattle, on property it doesn't own. Nor can it prevent the conversion of rangeland to agricultural land; nor can it prevent prairie dogs from being poisoned on adjacent land.

Heck, it might not even be able to retain jurisdiction over the property it has.

"Want to talk about the army's designs on the Timpas tract?" I asked.

We didn't find any sign of the tornado. Evidence of the storm brewing over the Timpas section of the Comanche Grassland is likewise obscure, but the impact is potentially far, far greater.

DESERT MANEUVERS

Tom didn't have to address the question. He's a career civil servant, nearing retirement. The issue, while still wide open, was going to be decided at a higher level than his desk. But as the district ranger in charge of one of North America's most wonderfully intact grassland ecosystems (and as your servant), he had both the standing to be aware and the cause to be disturbed.

Although stronger words might be found.

As Tom explained, the Fort Carson military base has ambitions to add 240,000 acres to its training area. Incorporated into the acquisition area is 190,000 acres of the Comanche Grassland—essentially the entire Timpas tract. The military did, in fact, once own the land. They divested themselves of it in 1991 and gave it to the Forest Service. In addition to the grasslands environment, the area is celebrated for its rich prehistoric and archaeological treasures (most notably Native American pictographs and an array of dinosaur tracks) and for the rugged and beautiful Picket Wire Canyonlands—a popular hiking and horseback riding trail system.

The army, apparently, wants it in order to train more troops for desert warfare and zero in their artillery to hit targets about a time zone away.

I say "apparently" because no formal request or notification had been made from the army to the Forest Service. Tom found out about it through a *Denver Post* reporter who called out of the blue one day in the autumn of 2006 to ask District Ranger Peters what he thought about the army's map.

"What map?" said Tom.

"I'll fax it to you," said the reporter, who then called back.

"Now what do you think?" he asked.

Tom probably didn't say what he thought, and he didn't tell me what he said. What he did say with regard to the army's designs was that, as far as he was concerned, the Forest Service was "the right agency to manage these lands for the public good."

A fair number of people who fall under the public banner apparently agree. On the way into La Junta, the closest large town to the controversy, is a hand-painted sign that says: "KEEP THE ARMY OUT OF PICKET WIRE." On the trailhead sign-in sheet for Vogel Canyon Picnic Area, there were three notations in the "Comment" areas that read: "Please keep the army out of here."

Okay, admittedly this is not a representative sampling of public opinion. But I haven't heard your opinion. And you own the place.

Funny, isn't it, how the overlooked value of a place goes up when someone wants to take it from you. And who would have guessed that a fully mechanized army, which hasn't had a horse pulling a caisson in nearly one hundred years, would come around, once again, to needing grass?

Burning Desire

We arrived at last, and finally, at a large burn area that Tom and his crew had burned only four weeks earlier. I think our visit was just the excuse Tom needed to see how things were progressing. I think, for a grassland manager, watching the vegetative recovery of a successful burn is as affirming as watching the crops a farmer sows germinating in the tilled soil.

"Look. Over there," Tom directed. "Look how the grass is coming up. Fan-tas-tic!" he pronounced.

"Look. Over here. You see how this sand sage is totally charred and this one, a foot away is barely touched and . . .

"Look. Over there. That yucca isn't even touched. The whole area wasn't touched. The fire swept right around it."

Just as fire did and does, naturally, in nature. Not only does fire not destroy the native vegetation (contrary to the proselytizing of Smokey Bear) but it prunes it selectively and judiciously. Just as rainfall is not uniform—heavy here, lighter down the street, absent in the next town—fire burns some areas thoroughly, others lightly, others not at all.

It wasn't just coincidence that the only Cassin's sparrow in the burn area was smack in the middle of an unburned plot, just as it wasn't coincidence that horned larks were already nesting in a heavily burned area. Cassin's sparrows like tallgrass, and their outpost was destined to be surrounded by a lush sea of burn-spurred grasses in the next few weeks. Horned larks are partial to very sparsely vegetated habitat. The burn was made to order for them, and the larks' penchant for early nesting ensured that their breeding cycle would remain just ahead of the vegetative recovery.

Maybe it was because I was focused. Maybe it was because the burn was more recent and the recovery not so advanced. But I could finally see what Tom was seeing and was so excited about. The curious capriciousness of the fire. Burn this, spare this. Quick recovery here, slower recovery there. It was like the prairies themselves, a complex mosaic of plants, plant communities, and the animals that are, in unified sum, both sustained and sustaining.

But you had to look close. You had to get down in the dirt and look. Grasslands are no drive-by environment, no place for windshield tourists. You won't see a horned lizard at sixty-five miles an hour or be able to find spring flowers rising like the phoenix on its five hundredth or watch a Swainson's hawk hunt, on foot at the edge of a burn, or listen to the plaintive, pure-toned song of Cassin's sparrow.

You have to get out of the car and get out into it. Just as I was doing, now. Staring with newly kindled wonder at the fire-purified earth, seeing less and less the charred yucca and more and more the new grasses and flowers that were bursting through the soil.

My soil! My grasslands. So long as nobody appropriates them. And the best part is, I don't even have to maintain them. The largest agency within the Department of Agriculture is already doing that for me.

Just like Tom said, the hardest thing is finding and keeping good people. Lucky he's working for us. Unbelievable that more people don't come out here to see their national grasslands (and Tom's handiwork) firsthand.

On my way back to the car, it occurred to me that maybe what the Forest Service has here is a marketing problem. Just as the old Forest Service policy of blanket fire suppression is outmoded, maybe what grasslands need is their own totemic mascot. An animal at home in the grasslands and in sync with fire management—Backfire the Badger, Pyro Pete the Prairie Dog, or Combustible Coyote, who dashes through the underbrush with his tail on fire starting patchwork burns.

What does a bear in dungarees have to do with prairies, anyway?

Then it occurred to me that one of the hardest challenges on the planet is getting an organization or institution to change its cherished symbols. It would be easier to get the army to give up its designs on the Comanche Grassland or convince Mount Rushmore–bound tourists that there is more between the Mississippi River and Mount Rushmore than rest stops than it would be to get the Forest Service to give up Smokey Bear.

But for the record, I still like the Combustible Coyote idea.

Does anybody know a good marketing firm that wants to take on the high-profile challenge of selling grasslands to the people who own them?

Johnny Earth Day

He was walking along Colorado County Road 802 and heading in our direction, a slight, spry marionette dressed in blue running shorts and a red runner's shirt, and carrying a big white industrial-strength trash bag. My first thought was Tom Bombadil of Lord of the Rings fame. My second was Johnny Appleseed. Both fell short.

We were parked, make that poised, at the turnoff to the Vogel Canyon Picnic Area and in the middle of a discussion relating to road conditions and the efficacy of proceeding farther.

I was for going on. Linda, in the process of scooping mud out of the rear wheel wells with her hands, was inclined to wait until the roadbed dried. Her well-considered argument had reached a point just short of exhuming past instances when her prudent council had been ignored (and we got to test the reliability of our RV roadside service policy) when she realized that I was no longer listening but was, instead, staring fixedly off toward the west.

"What are you looking at?" she demanded.

"I don't know," I answered truthfully.

Curious now, she peered around the rear of the van and pursed her lips.

"I see your problem," she agreed.

"Then you see it, too?"

"Skinny guy in shorts carrying a big white sack and moving like a high-scoring pinball?"

"Uh-huh. Any thoughts?"

There was a brief period of silence, which became a protracted period of silence, during which time we watched the figure approach quickly and steadily except for the occasional tacking foray to the side of the road, where he stopped and apparently found something he wanted. I searched the horizon for a car. Seeing none, I scanned overhead for a spaceship.

"What's out in that direction?" I asked.

"Prairie," she replied. "About thirty miles of it."

"Seems like a pretty unlikely place to run into a street person," I observed.

"Can't be a street person," Linda assessed. "No shopping cart."

"Could be the mud," I postulated. "Cart might be mired up to the axles just over the hill."

"Might," she said. "Glad to know you're seeing my point."

There was another period of silence, during which the figure put down his bag and walked, somewhat jerkily and purposefully, out onto the prairie, where he stopped to pick up something that glinted in the light, which he then carried back to the road and deposited in the bag.

"I'd say he was collecting cans," Linda concluded, and this it turned out was mostly true. I learned later that, owing to their tendency to tear through most plastic trash bags, bottles were usually (if somewhat regrettably) ignored. But roadside paper and plastic trash were well within jurisdictional bounds, and I was, over the course of the next several hours, destined to learn that the gentleman's current trash route included Florida, Alabama, Mississippi, Louisiana, Texas, New Mexico, and Colorado. Last year his roadside collection service had operated in California, Oregon, Idaho, Wyoming, and Montana.

"Happy Earth Day!" he chanted as he drew within heralding distance, then tacked off into the prairie to retrieve a discarded Coors Light can that was mostly hidden beneath a cluster of tumbleweeds.

"Guy's got great eyes," I assessed. Which he clearly did, with the assistance of a set of thickish-lensed glasses. It was tough to make out his features, hidden as they were behind about three weeks' growth of beard and beneath a sun-blocking French legionnaire's hat. His mouth seemed perpetually poised to treat the world to his smile. His magnified eyes shifted between wide-eyed openness and a squint.

It might have been the hat, or the glasses, or his jerky animation, but he recalled to me, suddenly, Dustin Hoffman playing the role of the exiled master counterfeiter in the movie *Papillon*. But it might have been his detachment, too, his returned focus on trash without any follow-up to his Earth Day greeting. As I watched, our Earth Day celebrant shifted the bag to his other shoulder and turned the corner, heading toward the campground, which was a good two miles away. So much for his immediate point of origin.

"Mind if I walk with you a bit?" I asked.

I learned that he was forty-eight years old before learning his name. That he used to work for a midwestern university. Had a job doing something in the computer lab and was the last "to be let go."

He used to go home for Christmas. He loved music and had a collection of vinyl records he kept at the house of a friend. His birthday was June 3. He celebrated it the day after he was shot by a turkey hunter in Texas. He needed to be back in Michigan in June for his thirtieth high school reunion.

All these disclosures took much more time to glean than to recount. The fellow had a world-class stutter, and when his eyes spied some can or bottle, his focus often brought conversation to a halt until his prize could be subdued and bagged.

Yes. I said bottle. The usually operational bottle embargo had been lifted for Earth Day, and one of the things this did was to make the bag he was carrying weigh a ton. I know. I helped carry it.

"Huh," he said, after exhuming a half-buried bottle from its sandy resting place, followed by the detached label, which read, "Fresca." "You don't find many Frescas," he observed. "I always think of snow when I find one."

And if you are able to make the cognitive juxtaposition linking Fresca and snow, it means two things. You watched too many TV commercials when you were a kid. And you've got a mind whose insulation is badly worn or missing, just like my new friend, whom I nicknamed Johnny Earth Day.

By the way, I got the Fresca-snow connection immediately.

"You must get to find some odd things at times," I prompted, leaving the nature of those things open to the imagination. He chose to stick to the subject of bottles.

"Oh, o-o-o-o-oh yee; Oh o-o-o-yee; Oh-o-o-o Yeah!" he affirmed. "W-w-w-w-one time I f-f-f-found a-a-a Fay . . . a Fay . . . a Faygo bottle in T-T-T-Texas!"

Clearly I'd hit upon a favorite subject. His stutter seemed to increase in measure with his enthusiasm.

Faygo, I learned, is a "pop" that is apparently indigenous to Michigan and that Johnny Earth Day was fond of "twenty years ago." In a series of lateral skips and jumps, the conversation moved on to regional names for soft drinks.

All "pop" is called "coke" in the South and "soda" in the Northeast.

Then a recounting of the time his (high school?) coach got the (cross-country?) team lost in western New York. Then to the twelve to fourteen pairs of running shoes he had in his van (not one the same make or model) and not thirteen pairs, either. Twelve to fourteen!

"L-l-l-like t-t-t-tall, t-t-t-tall, t-t-t-tall buildings," he explained. "N-n-n-no thir-thir-thir-thirteenth floor."

I confess I didn't immediately get the point of the twelve to fourteen disclosure and architectural superstitions. By this time the needle on my internal "weirdo-meter" was pegged in the yellow zone, still well short of red, but it wasn't until my acquaintance picked up and then gently resettled a piece of presumed trash that was, in reality, a shattered shard of the Forest Service's boundary marker, that I began to really appreciate how much strain there was on the linchpins of this guy's logic.

"How come you didn't pick up that piece of plastic?" I asked.

"Because it's government property, and the warning label said not to remove or destroy. Like the labels on mattresses," he explained. "You can't remove them, either."

"Oh," I said. "How did you find this campground?" I asked, as much from honest curiosity as to change the subject.

"I uh, I uh, I uh ha-ha-have a book th-th-that tells me where fr-fr-free camping grounds are."

And he did. I saw it on the dashboard of his car. A car whose interior looked like a hamper but whose registration was not only current but recently renewed.

It turned out he was shot by the turkey hunter because he was on his way to get his Michigan registration renewed in some way, shape, or fashion in Texas. I guess it worked.

The campground guide was well thumbed. Well used.

The U.S. Forest Service and the Bureau of Land Management commonly do not charge camping fees in their primitive camping areas. This is a boon for travelers on tight budgets and for people who have struck their own curious balance with life. If you frequent these campgrounds, as Linda and I do, you get to see quite a cross section of interesting people.

"Y-y-y-ya know," Johnny observed. "If-f-f-f everyone went out and p-p-p-picked up cans j-j-just once a year—just once in their life!"—he corrected himself—"n-n-n-nobody would litter."

It's true. I'm certain of it. Because at the time my newest friend made this observation, it was my turn to carry the bag, and it was, as we neared the campground, getting pretty close to sixty pounds. Pretty hard penance to pay for other people's sloppiness. But I only helped. He was the guy bearing the weight of the cross.

"D-d-d-do you h-h-have a current n-n-newspaper?" he asked. "W-w-w-one with comics?"

I told him we did, and that he was welcome to it. "Sports page, too."

Not wanting to take a chance that we might decide not to risk driving the Road Pig down the muddy road, he walked back with me. Another four miles round trip (not that that means much to a runner). Now that I'd won his confidence, he got down to the serious business of telling me his life's story.

"All my life I've had two answers for every question," he

said, as if this disclosure were something new, something I couldn't have guessed. Then, perhaps predictably:

"Have you read Hermann Hesse?" Then:

"Have you read Ayn Rand?" Then:

"I'd like to write a book about my travels, my experiences, and my philosophy for life. Do you know any books like that, that have already been written?"

I didn't have the heart to tell him about *Blue Highways*. But since we were now somewhat retro-calibrated, I told him he might want to consider *Zen and the Art of Motorcycle Maintenance* as a possible literary rival.

"Ya-ya-ya know," he confided from that great depth of intimacy that only the sharing of sixty pounds of other people's garbage can confer upon two people, "I've always b-b-b-been juh-juh-just a little out of sy-sy-sy-sy-sy-sync with other people."

I told him I could relate.

We didn't see a single can or bottle on the way back to our van. The guy was a real pro.

And the next morning, when he went off on his run, he really did have on a different pair of running shoes. I didn't ask what number they were in the lineup, but I'm sure he would have told me. All I know for certain is that they weren't number thirteen.

Funny, the people you meet doing public service in the middle of nowhere. But then, Forest Service grasslands are open to everyone and "everyone" is pretty all-inclusive. Given the "carry in, carry out" policy, which some people tend to ignore, it's sure nice when some person comes along and picks up the trash.

I think the next one will be me. I hope the one after that will be you.

And no, I don't know how often Johnny Earth Day makes his rounds. I forgot to ask. He didn't say.

So it might be up to you and me. Neither of us has to wait until Earth Day to take up the cross. Whether you care to leave the bottles and just do cans is entirely up to you.

Chapter 8
Picture Canyon

You come upon the canyon suddenly, but not because the delineation between open prairie and flanking rock walls is abrupt. It's not. First the road descends. Then ahead of you it climbs, but before you appreciate the topographic implications of this . . .

Ah. There it is. The sign to the canyon turnoff. You go right. Keeping your eyes fixed ahead, on your destination, searching for the promised canyon walls that lie only a mile ahead (according to the brochure). Just around a bend. Maybe the next.

Only when you finally see the vertical cliffs rising before you do you realize that the canyon has trapped you already. The hills have closed around and grown toothy with rocks. The flanking grasslands that appeared so open and inviting were only window-dressing—side-window-dressing. Your attention focused ahead, you never noticed as the horizon drew closer and the grasslands became squeezed to grass and scrabble edge.

You have been beguiled by the land. Now you are trapped. Leave now, or become enchanted.

Visitors, going back thousands of years, have suffered that fate. Few who come here escape unscathed.

There is something about canyons that draws you on just as they guide you in. Walls that get higher and steeper. Colors and patterns that get richer and more vibrant. The promise of more ahead. What? You don't know. Why? You don't ask.

Not yet.

So you continue, coming finally to a parking area. Three shaded picnic pavilions. A toilet. A trailhead sign-in. A gate. If you want to see the treasures of the canyon, you'll have to walk from here.

Most visitors, I'm delighted to say, do. Fewer visitors, I'm sorry to say, than the canyon deserves. On an average Sunday in spring, the ravens and American kestrels and great horned owls that roost in the shadow-cloaked ledges above the toilet would be shocked to count more than a dozen cars.

Beguiling it might be. Overused, Picture Canyon is not. And you might be wondering why a book devoted to the subject of prairie grasslands is making a dodge into a canyon at all. The answer is, it's not—that is, my focus on canyons is thematically apt. Canyons are integral elements of the prairie environment. Seams in the grassy skin of the earth that add character and biological diversity. Picture Canyon, nestled deep in the Comanche Grassland, is a picture-perfect example.

It began, long ago, as undifferentiated as the prairie itself. A seabed transmuted into rock (I told you there was magic here), topped off with a layer of volcanic sealant, glossed over with a layer of dirt and a glaze of grass. At some point the earth below shifted or shrugged (or perhaps when all the layers were laid there was some flaw in the horizontal symmetry or a misappropriation of materials and supply). For whatever reason, some part of the earth's surface was lower than the flanking plain's, and water, being water, found it a convenient place to go.

At this point, where the water went is less important than what it did, and what it did was to wear a little groove in the earth that cut down through the deposits of gravel and sand until it came to the hard, volcanic layer that protected the old seabed the way enamel protects the soft body of your teeth.

Water is patient and tenacious stuff. Having no place to go but down, in time it cut a path through the hard cap rock, down to the sandy dentin below, and then it really went to work. Wearing away layer after layer of fossil seabed the way psychologists probe the layers of your psyche. Exposing the rippled depositions along ever-widening sides and deepening cliffs. Over millions of years it turned a gulch into a canyon—one hundred yards wide at its narrowest point, half a mile at the widest, with cliffs towering seventy to two hundred feet above the canyon floor where, naked against the wind, they were sculpted into eye-catching and gravity-defying shapes and forms.

If you stand on the Picture Canyon floor, you can see the dark layer of cap rock encircling the canyon like the rusty rim of a can—an analogy that is as apt as it is descriptive. If you pick up a chunk of cap rock, and since the stuff litters the canyon floor you won't have trouble finding some—you cannot help but appreciate its weight. The volcanic flue that spouted the stuff must have tapped into one iron-rich pool of magma. This ferric content accounts for the color as well as the weight. Allowing for a geographic kink or two, the canyon runs pretty much north and south and straddles state boundaries. Two miles past the parking lot, you'll find a weathered sign announcing Oklahoma. A barbed wire fence reinforces this jurisdictional shift as well as a transition from public to private land.

There is, in addition to the main canyon, a series of side canyons, cut by their own delinquent trickles of water, adding their own special character, and offering footing for several popular hiking trails that lead up, out, and then back to the parking area. But as it was in the beginning, it is the water (not the watercourse) that is the canyon's guiding attraction, along with the vegetation water supports and the microclimate such vegetation helps create.

The side canyons offer shade and footing for junipers. Some of the deeper, more sheltering gorges are home to micro-woodlands—linear stands of ancient junipers with twisted trunks, and gnarly-barked cottonwoods, whose roots point the way to water. Mule deer frequently pass through and sometimes bed here. Great horned owls roost. On the cliffs, rock squirrels go about the business of squirrels who shun trees, pack rats wait out the day in nooks and crannies, and cold-blooded reptiles like collared lizards and rattlesnakes find the right balance of sun and shade to keep body temperatures regulated.

On the floor of the main canyon, at its widest point, there is a small pond, rimmed with cattails and cottonwoods and smaller pools, protected from the desiccating effects of the sun by flanking boulders and the bracketing cliffs. This oasis was almost certainly the primary attractant for the canyon's earliest human visitors, native peoples who came for the promise of water and to hunt the animals who were likewise drawn.

These people were, like the bison they hunted, nomadic, but while their affinity for this place shied from permanence, it seems anchored in spiritual meaning, because they left behind, on the water-smoothed cliffs, pictures and carvings that may still be seen today. Pictures of animals they were familiar with, pictures of people they knew.

On the western side of the canyon is Crack Cave, a narrow fissure whose angle aligns perfectly with the rays of the sun on June 21—the last day of spring, the first day of summer. The pictographs on the cave's walls have been dated back a thousand years, and on the longest day of the year, and only this day, they are illuminated.

Only a fool would call this a coincidence.

They came for water and for shelter, these first visitors. They found something else. Something important enough to mix colors (which came from nature) with artistic skill (which comes from the mind and the soul) and commit it to stone.

For those who came later to see and appreciate, and, maybe, to try to understand. If they failed, it's because they framed their expectations poorly, believing that what the pictures might show them was an answer. If they succeeded, it's because they carried their understanding with them and found it mirrored in the canyon.

The pictures are just a portal.

You wondered, earlier, why a book about the prairies would concern itself with canyons, and I think I answered by saying that canyons are, in fact, simply part of the prairie ecosystem—and this is true. But I might have offered a different explanation. Like my friend Johnny Earth Day, I sometimes find myself trapped between answers, and it occurs to me, now, that the other answer, the one I didn't offer, was the better answer after all. Here it is:

If you were to sit on the rim of the canyon, plant your seat on rocks that many a contemplative person has sat on before, your eyes would fall upon a beautiful flat plain covered by platinum-colored grass, and delicate flowers, and sage that perfumes the air with mind-clearing scents, and you'd suddenly realize that it looks much like the prairie two hundred feet above and all around you.

What you see below is what you'll see above, and vice versa.

The canyon, at least this canyon, is just a prairie in a geologic terrarium where it is easy to appreciate and easy to behold. It isn't part of the prairie ecosystem. It is the prairie ecosystem. And the prairie ecology is it.

Perhaps the biggest problem with prairies, and people's ability to appreciate them, is their scale. It all just seems too big. So complex. So incomprehensible. So . . . vast.

Like life.

Maybe the way to get a handle on the awesome totality is to start with a little sliver, a little sample of the universe, set between flanking walls of stone, where our myopia is not a factor.

Someplace like a canyon. Picture Canyon. A prairie within a prairie, where people come to see the writing on the wall.

TALKING HORSE

I executed a side step through the Forest Service gate—a design contrived to confound cattle and horses—and made my way toward the canyon wall, glowing in the light of the late afternoon sun. I might have chosen the western, sheltered side. The view there is equally fine.

Snug against the cliffs, there is a crumbling foundation, made of double-walled stone, that once housed some family of nesters, very probably the canyon's original European settlers. The site is close to water, the location well chosen for the view and the warming touch of winter sunlight when all else in the canyon would still be in shadow.

But however well situated or constructed, the walls could not wall out the harsh realities of prairie life. Like so many other settlers in Baca County, the nesters "starved out." Some yellowing, boxed, and basement-stored tax ledger in Springfield might contain their names. The crumbling stone walls speak only to their anonymous past presence.

I chose the east side. Mostly for the view of what was working up to be a beautiful evening. Maybe even a magical one! I know some people scoff at the idea of magic. A childish notion, they say. Fairy tales and whimsy at best. Me? I like to keep an open mind. Unlike other institutions I once put my childhood faith in, magic, at least, has never let me down.

The cliff was a veritable sandstone bleacher, with every seat still available for the matinee. Some with, some without backrests. Some shaded, some not. Every one of them offered an orchestra pit view of the canyon and the sky.

Well, almost every one. The first rock I picked had a cottonwood crowding the view to the southwest. It was bound to block a guiding star or two.

I moved one, then two boulders to the right, realizing, suddenly, that the one I'd settled upon was next to the canyon's most celebrated attraction. The pictograph drawing of a horse. Its redrawn image graces the Forest Service brochure, and a photo hangs on the wall of the Lamar Chamber of Commerce.

"Sorry," I said to the image, because I was feeling uninhibited enough to talk to a painting. "Can you see over my head?"

The horse didn't answer, and there could be several reasons for this. (You'd have to be very arrogant to conclude that there was only one.) Maybe the animal was deep in thought or so used to being treated as an object that it was surprised to be addressed.

Maybe it was deaf (as stone?), or maybe it didn't understand English.

The artist who painted it was Native American; possibly a Comanche, the next-to-last people to be run off the land. Or maybe one of an earlier native peoples the Comanche displaced. Only one thing was certain. The pictograph was not very old. Horses were reintroduced to the New World by the Spanish. While native people were on the grassland perhaps as early as eleven thousand years ago, the first time they might have seen a horse was 1540, when Coronado's horse-mounted soldiers passed this way. The horse culture of the prairie Indians flourished for only three hundred years.

So while the horse might have understood one or more of the dialects spoken by the native peoples of the plains, and it might have understood Spanish, it's unlikely that it would have picked up much English. And let's not overlook the fact that real horses don't speak (not that this limitation must automatically apply to painted horses that are very probably magical).

I prefer to think that the horse didn't answer because it was shy, and I draw this conclusion from the depiction itself. Just look at the posture, the body language. Slender on to willowy. A neck like Audrey Hepburn's. Head turned demurely down. Shy . . . or maybe haughty. The animal was, after all, famous.

And beautiful. In just a few carefully cut lines, the artist had captured the elemental elegance of an animal born to race the wind across lands where the wind has never known a rival. Linda and I had been on the prairies almost six weeks now and had come to respect the power of prairie wind. But my money was on the horse.

"Mind if I call you Bill?" I asked. "I know that's not your real name, but I don't speak Comanche, so do you have any problem with Bill?"

The horse didn't seem to mind at all.

"My name's Hieronymus Bosch," I lied. "Come from the Garden of Earthly Delights," I lied even more. "One of your biggest fans."

Bill seemed to take all this in stride.

"So how does it feel being a celebrity? The talk of Picture Canyon. The horse cut in stone, imprinted on a thousand hearts."

The horse let its fame, or its modesty, speak for itself.

"I mean, how do you respond to people who travel hundreds, even thousands of miles, and walk half a mile down a sun-cooked canyon, just to look at you. And run their fingers over your lines. And strain to see something in you, in this wall, that nobody has ever seen before?"

It was a lot to respond to, and I'm not surprised Bill chose not to.

"Or let's look at this another way," I suggested. "Put the cart in front of the horse. Have you ever wondered why people come down here? Not art lovers. Not history buffs. Not archaeologists. People. Just plain ordinary people."

Like me, I might have added, but didn't.

"They come all the way down here. When they could just pick up the brochure or maybe download your image from the Forest Service website, or catch you on The History Channel in the comfort of their home entertainment center."

While I was speaking, the light seemed to go out of the wall, and image shuddered into shadow. Nothing supernatural, I assure you. It was just the sun slipping behind the western rim, turning the canyon into a vessel of evening. It was just one world dissolving into another. Happens all the time. Twice a day, in fact.

"I'll give you a minute to think about that," I said to Bill, and I did. Turned my back on the painting and my face toward the sky, which was beginning to be softened by a peach-colored blush. The wind, which had made the delicate new leaves on the canyon's cottonwoods shiver and whisper, was gone. Except for the sassing song of a rock wren and the soulful lament of mourning doves, the canyon was silent.

I don't know what it is about sunsets that captivates us.

Yes, certainly color. But isn't the transitory nature of sunrises and sunsets part of the allure, too?

Daylight, which is our species' primary activity period, spans thirteen or more hours in this latitude in spring. We get to see a lot of daylight during our time on this planet.

Night is when we shut the world out and turn inward, into dreams that ferry us across the dark hours. In the dark, they seem as vivid as life. Before morning, they cast an exit spell, leaving only the outline of a memory that every morning as we wake we struggle to recall.

Have you ever wondered why? Why day-spawned memories are so vivid but night memories are so elusive? I have.

But for a brief time, twice each day, our two worlds are bridged. Day and night, reality and dreams—they mix and mate at dawn and dusk. Reality, in these between times, seems not so concrete; dreams, during these intervals, not so elusive.

Even questions and answers seem not so different or apart.

As the shadows began to fill the valley, I found myself staring at the foundation of the nesters' home on the far side of the valley, the side the shadows claimed first. I found myself wondering: Who were they? Where did they come from? How long had they lived here? When and where did they go?

Did some of them never leave?

And since the failure of their ambitions was self-evident, it begged the greater questions: What possessed them to come here? Why would anyone pin hopes upon such a harsh, lonely, naked environment? I found myself feeling curiously akin to these failed nesters. We both, after all, shared an affinity for this canyon, one separated only by time. We also shared, being of the same species, similar needs and ambitions. In this, and in our need for understanding, we were one.

It occurred to me that Bill could have answered these questions, but he was already on assignment. Then it occurred to me that maybe the questions were not unrelated.

"Hold that thought," I said. "Maybe we'll get back to it. In the meantime, how about telling me about the people who used to live over there? A little collaborative effort. I'll flesh out a story line; you fill in the blanks. You can be primary author."

The horse greeted this proposal with agreeable silence.

"Okay," I said. "Just tell me if I'm wrong."

I looked hard at the ruins, first because there were important truths to unearth there; second because, in the growing twilight, shadows and the forms that cast them were getting harder to separate.

There were two buildings. One that seemed to be the house; the other, perhaps, a barn. Both made of stone. The house had a smaller room off to the side.

"Married couple," I said. "Young. Strong. Much in love. Of course they wanted a measure of privacy."

Nothing from Bill. Not a snort, not a neigh.

"Kids," I added. "A bunch. Boys and girls. All about a year apart."

Affirmative silence.

"Some died young. Accident, childhood diseases."

Respectful silence.

Broke their hearts, I knew and didn't need to say.

Utter silence.

The sky was getting darker. The peachy blush was gone. The wren had stopped his chatter. Only the mourning doves remained. Calling from the cliffs beyond the cottonwoods, the cottonwoods that rimmed the pond that was the centerpiece of the canyon, mirroring the land and the sky.

"They raised cattle!" I said, I knew. It explained the excavated pond. "And put forty acres under the plow. Down here, in the valley."

The horse didn't need to respond to these suppositions. They were self-evident. Most nesters, in order to fulfill the obligations of tenancy, put 40 of their 160 acres under the plow. As for cattle, the family in the canyon was a long way from a railhead or a town. Wheat had to be transported. Cattle could walk to market. So long as there was a market, so long as there was grass and water to sustain cattle. So long as the forces of the universe didn't abruptly and inexplicably turn against them.

"They starved out in the thirties."

The odds and the silence said yes. Baca County went from eight thousand to four thousand souls during the Dust Bowl. It ranked among the hardest hit areas to be touched by the drought.

"But this family lasted longer than most, lasted a long

time," I said, not even waiting for silence. "They were good people, and young, and strong, and they gave it all they had from stubbornness, and pride, and the love and support they gave to each other."

"They were good people," I said, again. A judgment I make of most people, and this, another article of faith left over from childhood, has not let me down.

The first stars were beginning to appear. Venus, obvious and bright. One . . . two . . . peeking through the gathering darkness. Now, three and four . . . More if I didn't focus my gaze directly, searched the heavens from the corners of my eyes. It's curious how it's easier to see the stars if you don't look at them directly. It has something to do with the location of the optic nerve, they tell me, but it's curious nevertheless.

It was curious, too, but I couldn't seem to get my bearings, couldn't pin names to stars that I have been on a first-name basis with for years. Maybe it was because I was in the canyon and so couldn't see the whole sky, couldn't get my bearings. Maybe it was still too early and my senses were muddled by twilight.

But Venus, the Evening Star, or Anpo Wicahpi, the "Morning Star," of the Lakota Sioux, was bright, and affirming, and beautiful by any measure applied by heaven or earth.

"Wait," you say. "How can a planetary body be both a morning and an evening star?"

Hold that thought. We'll get back to it. Right now, I'm interviewing a magical horse.

"In the evening," I continued. "After the winds had dropped. After the chores were done. After the children were put to bed, they would come out and sit to savor the silence, wouldn't they?"

Bill honored the truth with silence.

"They sat here!" I said, I knew, in some way more fundamental than mere understanding. "It was a short walk. They could see the house. They could talk in private—about their cares and concerns, what they'd done during the day, what they hoped to do tomorrow.

"They would come out here," I continued, "and they would have some time together. And when all the saying was said, they'd sit, for a time, and savor the sunset, just like I am doing now, until the first stars appeared. Then, before it got too dark to see the path, they'd return home, to their room on the side of the house, and . . .

"They had dreams," I said. And while it wasn't a question, I turned quickly toward Bill for an answer anyway.

And Bill blinked.

You wouldn't have seen it unless you were looking at him. I might not have seen it if I'd been a hair quicker or a tad slower and hadn't caught the movement just out of the corner of my eye. It was like the shadow of an owl crossing the moon that is gone before you bring your head up. It was like the image that lingers and dies in your mind the instant you open your eyes—too vivid to be a dream, too elusive to be trapped by memory.

It wasn't a trick of light, and it wasn't the play of shadows. It was as real as the dying sunset, which is both a bridge and a wedge between day and night, dream and reality. It surprised me, too. The blink, not the realization. Of course they had dreams! Who doesn't? And they changed and grew just as we do.

When we are young, our dreams are filled with possibility—some alluring enough to pursue in the light of day, some frightening enough to make us get under our beds and hide. But when we grow older, our dreams become populated by memories of things that were and people we knew—friends and family, who become more real at night than daytime memories can make them.

And it's funny, but the older I get the more I look forward to bedtime. Not because I'm tired, but because at night I am surrounded once again by people I have known and loved. The Plains Indians believed it was so, that the spirits of the dead, who otherwise resided in the Milky Way, the "spirit path" (the galaxy we live in), visit us in our dreams. They believed, too, that the earth below was perfectly mirrored by the spirit world above—in somewhat the same way that this canyon is like and part of the prairie above and around it. What you find down here, you find up there.

There was symmetry in the way the native people regarded the universe. There was balance. There was no discord, not even much distinction between spirit and matter, because down here and up there were, in fact, one and the same.

And yes, I know that our dreams are supposed to be products of our imagination, a way of organizing and filing away life's experiences to help us relate to the world around us. Fair enough. But that doesn't preclude the possibility that dreams may also be bridges to the universe, to help us sort the universe out and find our place there, too.

Well does it?

Back to Venus. The Morning and Evening Star. The thought you've been holding. There is actually no discord between the dual labels, and there should be little room for confusion. Like Earth, Venus is a planet orbiting the sun, not a star, so unlike the stars, it will not always appear in the same place, at the same time, year after year. Sometimes in its orbit, Venus appears above or ahead of the daily path of the sun. Sometimes it lies below the sun or trailing behind. So at times, and for a period of several months, Venus will appear before the sun appears in the morning sky, becoming the Morning Star. Sometimes it trails the sun, so it lingers in the evening sky after the sun has set, becoming, then, the Evening Star.

While Venus's position has much to do with where it is in relation to the sun, there is one other key element involved here. That is Earth. Where Venus appears, relative to the sun, has much to do with where it is relative to us. If we were viewing Venus from, say, the planet Mercury, our perspective of our sister planet would be very, very different. (Very short-lived, given the surface temperature of the planet closest to the sun, but, different.)

It all comes down to perspective, and getting back to the discussion relating to dreams, while I am sure that the careful ponderings of an Austrian psychiatrist who wanted to kill his father and marry his mother are not without merit, I'm not willing to preclude the possibility that the Plains Indians' sense of spirituality didn't tap into something greater than my limited insights or imagination—or Sigmund Freud's, either. If dreams are portals that look in, doesn't it just make sense that they are also portals to see out? Who ever said dreams are supposed to run only one way?

You want to call this sophistry? Fine. But the fact is I do get to talk with my old friends and relatives every night. And I've never enjoyed so much as a courtesy call from Sigmund Freud.

Now, please excuse me. I'm busy talking to a painted horse.

It was much darker, now. Poorwills were calling from up canyon and down. The three stars that make up Orion's belt were clearly visible, the same three stars that form the wrist of the constellation known to the Sioux as the Hand. With these stars to guide me, I was finally oriented enough to find my way across the sky. A little helping hand from the spirit world was all it took.

But the outline of the horse was barely visible now. It had become filled with shadow that made light of its graceful lines, running over them and up across the cliff face, spilling out across the canyon floor, blanketing the foundation of the nesters' house in darkness.

It was late. Past time to leave. Linda would be holding dinner. Sitting on the step of the RV. Watching the stars come out. Listening for the sound of steps that would herald my approach. I told her I'd be late. Still, she might be getting worried. There are worse things in the world than shadows under the bed—among them rattlesnakes and ankle-turning rocks that lie in paths.

"Listen, Bill," I said, "with apologies to you, I've got to go now. Got some thoughts I want to get on paper and a bunch of people I'm looking forward to seeing tonight.

"And listen, for the record, I think it's fantastic that people come down here just to look at you, and now that I've been thinking about it, I don't think it makes any difference whether they know why they come here or not.

"Maybe if they come down here with their questions, and they don't find answers, maybe it's because the difference between the question and the answer isn't all that great to begin with."

Bill didn't respond, and there could be several reasons for this, too. It was answer enough.

"You're a nice horse," I added. "The guy who carved you had a good hand."

There was no moon, wouldn't be for several hours, but Venus's light was enough to detect the outline of the trail. I reached the gate without incident, and when my feet found the main path, I turned back and looked at the cliff. A tall, dark face of stone almost indistinguishable from the sky above it, except that the sky held stars and the cliff did not.

You couldn't see Bill. Couldn't even tell where he'd been. Couldn't tell whether he was, in fact, still there or not. I wouldn't presume to know what painted horses, much less magical horses, do at night. After their lines are erased and they are no longer bridled to the earth.

Maybe he races along the Star Path beneath the spirit of the man who painted him. Maybe he visits the dreams of the grandchildren or great-grandchildren of the nesters who once lived here. Maybe he doesn't go anywhere at all, content to stay and graze about the canyon, which is, after all, just a manageable slice of all that is, so no less magical than anyplace else in the universe.

And as I walked back, I thought, too, about the animation I'd seen: that blink. Had I really seen it? Was it just my imagination? It's hard not to second-guess something like that.

Then it occurred to me that it might not have been a blink at all. It might have been a wink!

In that evening light, it would have been hard to distinguish a blink from a wink. And given the circumstances, a wink would have been far more likely.

It must have been a wink. As gestures from painted horses go, a wink is a lot easier to accept than a blink. But of course, and once again, a lot depends upon perspective.

CHAPTER 9
Pawnee National Grassland, Colorado

GRASS UNDER PRESSURE

The sedan vaulted the hill going about twice as fast as conditions warranted but at a speed on par with the mood of the driver.

"He's heading right at us!" Linda exclaimed, and there was no denying the accuracy of this observation. In fact, I looked forward to the aftermath of the anticipated collision, when I could ask the car's sole occupant, "Why?"

Just short of the point when such a discussion seemed inevitable, the vehicle swerved to the left and skidded to a stop (a tricky maneuver on a dirt road). Anticipating our escape, the driver took the two steps to my window faster than the door on his car could open and bang shut. He was a rawboned gentleman, already shouting, wearing the clothes he'd hung over the chair three nights running and an expression of undiluted anger.

I'm exaggerating a bit. The man's expression was mostly hidden behind a mustache so bushy I mistook it for a beard (bushy mustaches seem to be a Front Range affection), but there was no mistaking his frame of mind. In fact, his mustache was fairly vibrating with anger. The guy, whoever he was, was really pissed, and I'm afraid it didn't help his mood when I met his verbal assault with a mild-toned

"Excuse me?"

"I said," he growled, "are you throwing your trash on my property?"

Ah, I thought. Now I get it. Private property is one of the West's most sacred totems, and abusing property rights is close to a hanging offense. Since we were stopped on a public road, and not guilty of dumping trash on his or anyone's property, I felt confident on the one hand but anxious on the other. For all I knew, watching birds constituted a hanging offense in the guy's eyes, too.

"We're looking for mountain plover," I offered. "Have you seen any?"

The disclosure and the question seemed to throw him off balance, his anger momentarily sidetracked as he struggled to fit my unexpected response into the framework of our presumed guilt. Trapped in this cognitive muddle, his brain went back to the default setting: righteous indignation.

"You're not dumping garbage on my property, are you?" he demanded, again.

"No," I assured him, "we're fresh out." (I smiled to let him know this was a joke.) "Like I said, we're just looking for mountain plover. We ran into a local birder who told us this was a good spot."

Given that the area was well known among Colorado birders as the place to find this increasingly elusive prairie shore bird, I felt confident that the landowner must have seen birders before, and (so long as none had abused his property) the precedent would support our presence, actions, and benign intent.

Despite the fact that we were in an RV with New Jersey plates—possibly a hanging offense in itself.

My explanation seemed to mollify the guy. While he didn't immediately apologize for accosting us, he did offer an explanation.

"I've had a lot of trouble with RV people," he said. "Comin' out here and dumping their trash on my land. People with big, expensive RVs, bigger 'n yours. Happened twice now. My son saw you parked here and thought that's what you was doin'. He called me and I come down."

"I understand," I said, and I did. Nice, open land situated right off Colorado 14—a scenic and well-traveled RV route and shortcut from I-80 and I-76 to Rocky Mountain National Park. His was the first dirt road off of a dirt road (and still within sight of the highway). Easy, convenient, and in the minds of drivin'-through RVers, who were "boondocking" to save money, or who simply forgot to dump their trash when they left the RV park that morning, the middle of nowhere.

That great, empty expanse called the prairies. A landfill just waiting to happen.

"Just because people have money to buy expensive RVs doesn't mean they're intelligent or responsible," I noted.

He nodded. "I just wanted to let you know why I came at you like I did. People in Colorado are real friendly, and we like visitors, but we're tired of . . ."

I don't remember what pejorative label he chose.

Okay, I do. It was "asshole."

But no matter how he chose to label or frame his frustration, the fact is he was focusing only on the tip of a much larger iceberg. He was a rancher on the Front Range of Colorado, and this meant he was standing right in the path of the suburban juggernaut. Twenty-five miles from Greeley, forty miles from Fort Collins, there were "prairie mansions," four-hundred- to five-hundred-thousand-dollar homes popping up within sight of his farmhouse. There were developers approaching him with land offers that got bigger every year. There were . . .

"People problems," a Forest Service wildlife biologist we met said in knowing sum. The grassland adjacent to the Front Range of the Rockies, which incorporates the Pawnee National Grassland and my rancher friend's lands, lies closer to more people and more population centers than any other grassland. Challenges and conflicts increase exponentially where increasing numbers of people make demands upon the land and its resources. And human encroachment is only one of the growing challenges North

America's grasslands are facing or will face. Others include changing climate, falling aquifer levels, invasive plants and animals, increased agricultural demand, overgrazing, mineral exploitation, wind turbine projects, and Arbor Day.

Arbor Day? Sure. A day set aside to plant trees to soothe the view on the "barren" prairies. Trees in a dry and fire-pruned environment constitute an invasive species. Our species's suppression of fire and our penchant for surrounding our homes, towns, and parks with trees have made us the mortal enemies of prairie.

If prairie plants were asked to name the "Black Sabbath," it would be Arbor Day.

Not that I was thinking of all this stuff while I was listening to the unhappy plight of the put-upon rancher. I was just trying to be sympathetic to his problem and was anxious to renew our search for mountain plover. The birds once were common hereabouts. In 1989, on our first visit, Linda and I had seen numbers of them.

"If you want to see birds," my now fully mollified rancher friend (who it turns out was retired navy; who was once stationed in New Jersey; who used to drive his Z28 Camaro all over the New Jersey Pine Barrens back in the sixties) said, "you should take Road Forty-nine north. Goes all the way to the Wyoming line."

"Course you'll have to talk your way past several cattle guards," he added.

I nodded.

"That's a joke," he explained.

I nodded again. Subtle humor they practice hereabouts. Subtle as the beauty of the prairies.

We parted on good terms. He with the outstanding apology, we with sympathy and understanding for his plight and thanks for his recommendations.

We never did find plover. No surprise there.

CROW VALLEY—WHERE EAST (INCREASINGLY) MEETS WEST

The bird was keyed up on a tree beside Crow Creek—a double misnomer. Crows are not much in evidence on the Pawnee Grassland of Colorado (this is magpie country), and the creek has never held water, not in the twenty years I've been coming to the grasslands; not aboveground anyway. But the valley, and the Crow Valley Campground, through which the dry watercourse winds, does have trees. Lots of them. Watercourse-hugging cottonwoods and drought-resistant Siberian elms—an island of trees in an ocean of grass.

That's how birds of woodlands and woodland edge see it. The bird on the bush was a case in point. My binoculars confirmed what the silhouette (and habitat, and my expectations) suspected. A blue jay. The bird had not been present when Linda and I had visited the Pawnee in early February. But today, May 6, it was here, back from some more temperate region where it spent the winter. A true pioneer, this vocal and primarily eastern species has expanded across the prairie plains—and it is not an exception. In fact, it is part of a broad and accelerating biological trend exhibited by a number of eastern birds and mammals that are colonizing the vast, and once treeless, regions.

Therein lies the key and the dilemma. Before pioneer settlement, significant woodlands were found on only a small fraction of the prairie biome. They occurred mostly in the eastern transition zone between the forests and the prairies, and along major watercourses, and while the land area they covered was small and relatively insignificant, less than 1 percent of the prairie biome, their influence was not.

Riparian corridors and isolated groves have always served as important resting, foraging, and breeding areas for a variety of native mammals, birds, and insects. Acting as biological halfway houses for species that had not quite fully adapted to pure prairie life, prairie woodlands provided footing for birds such as Swainson's hawk, western screech-owl, red-shafted flicker, western wood-pewee, and Bullock's oriole, among other species.

The ability of these species to make it on the prairies was dependent upon trees. The presence of trees on the prairies was dependent upon water. Drought is the prairie's way of cleaning house, of turning even drought-resistant trees into deadwood. Fire also helped keep those pesky trees at bay. Grass flourishes in the face of fire; trees die. So between drought and fire, the prairies were kept mostly tree-free.

What trees there were, were largely limited to places

where there were dependable sources of water and where fire hazard was less—places like steep canyons, rocky ridge-tops, and tinder-scoured watercourses.

Then European settlers arrived, and the balance changed. First, and perhaps most significant, was the impact of farming. Tilled earth isn't combustible (even sod needs a bit of drying and coaxing), and as more and more land went under the plow, the threat of grass fires diminished. One result was woodland encroachment. You can see the evidence in aerial photos, or as you drive along the interstates—stands and pockets of trees where prairie once stood. You can walk a Nebraska field left fallow for two or three years and navigate around the bumper crop of knee-high, prairie-nullifying eastern red cedar coming up all around you.

In addition to fire suppression, an element of proactive planting also helped change the landscape. If Ma Nature works against forests on the prairies, our species works to promote them. We love trees! Plant them wherever we go. Nurture them, encourage them, and protect them from harm. When people buy their little subdivision dream houses on the prairies, the first thing they do is plant trees. When town planners want to offer residents a little corner of shady quiet or give a little class to residential streets, they plant trees—and not necessarily native trees, either.

While native trees are preferable to introduced species, any tree planted on open, high prairie constitutes an invasive, and it will still require more water than the High Plains can naturally support. Unless planted trees receive a water supplement, Ma Nature isn't going to have to enlist the services of a grass fire to make the point that trees don't belong here.

Our species's penchant for woody plants is not a twenty-first-century affectation. Shelterbelts of living trees to buffer homes from wind and snow are almost as much a part of prairie life as rural mail delivery. In fact, during the Dust Bowl years, Franklin Roosevelt toyed with the idea of planting a massive, north-to-south-running shelterbelt of trees to keep Oklahoma (and Colorado and Texas) from blowing east.

And it is certainly not a coincidence that Arbor Day (national go-out-and-plant-a-tree day) was conceived by an ardent tree-hugger in Nebraska. And let's not forget what is, perhaps, the greatest example of arboreal love (if not human hubris): the Nebraska National Forest—a crusade to convert open wasteland (prairie) to verdant forest. It was the vision of a utopian-minded botanist named Charles E. Bessey, who in 1890 began feverishly planting trees (mostly pines) near the town of Halsey, Nebraska. After his death in 1915, his efforts were continued, first by friends and fellow visionaries and later, during the 1930s, by the Civilian Conservation Corps. When it was all said and planted, almost twenty thousand acres of not-quite-self-sustaining forest was created on what used to be grassland. Today the forest has attracted and supports a variety of plants and animals that would not otherwise or naturally be found there.

Like the blue jay in Crow Valley. With all those Arbor Day-inspired woodlands being planted in town squares, and shelterbelts going up around farm and ranch houses, blue jays, and a fair number of eastern birds and mammals, saw a path opening before them through the Great American Desert and simply island-hopped their way across the prairies.

In addition to blue jays, in Crow Valley you can find eastern screech-owl and brown thrasher, two other primarily eastern birds. The trees and thickets support a healthy population of American robin, house wren, warbling vireo, orchard and Bullock's oriole, and spotted towhee. None of these species would be here unless there were trees.

From the standpoint of seeing more birds of different species, the leafing out of the prairies and the westward expansion of eastern birds is a good thing.

From the standpoint of maintaining viable populations of prairie-specialized birds, it is less of a good thing. In fact, among the ranks of bird species in decline, decreases in the populations of grassland birds have been more dramatic than those in any other group.

As grass goes, so go grassland birds. My blue jay, sitting within earshot of western kingbirds and western meadowlarks, is not just a pioneer. He is a bellwether. A herald announcing rapid and dramatic changes coming to a grassland near you.

Pawnee Spring Revisited: Something Old, Something New; Something Diminished, Something Renewed

"We're coming up on the turn," Linda announced. Unnecessarily, I might add. The reason I'd almost missed the turn on to Road 96, the old birding route, the day before was that I was thinking. The reason I was driving so fast now, was . . .

"Whoa, bucko," my copilot chastised as I successfully (I submit in my own defense) negotiated the turn into Murphy's Pasture without causing too many articles in the RV to shift or even the coffee in our go cups to slosh through the openings (very much).

"There was a truck on my bumper," I asserted more than allowed.

"Bertha is lying on the back seat," Linda chastised more than explained.

Bertha, AKA Big Bertha, is Linda's 500-millimeter Nikkor lens, her "baby," and she lavishes a mother's love and protectiveness upon it (which, given the cost of replacing the thing, is perfectly understandable).

The retort "Well then, you should have told me about Bertha" was on my lips, but that's where it stayed. We'd been on the road nearly two months now. One husband, one wife, and two big Labrador retrievers, all sharing a space whose dimensions wouldn't meet minimum standards for a high-security prison cell. On top of this trying proximity, we'd just endured three days of rainy spring weather that had sabotaged our efforts to explore one of our favorite places in the world.

On my first visit to the Pawnee National Grassland, back in 1985, when I was a single thirty-four-year-old, driving a friend's 280Z, I'd turned onto this road and was immediately enchanted: Love at first sight. It wasn't just the scale and scope of the landscape—unencumbered grass and sky that met at the horizon. It wasn't just the view of the snow-capped Rockies floating above the horizon seventy miles away. It wasn't just the verdant openness.

It was the volume and vibrancy of life! Everywhere I turned, everywhere I looked, there was movement and sound. Larks and longspurs rocketing skyward. Antelope loping over hilltops. Prairie dogs yipping. Thirteen-lined ground squirrels plunging for dens. Swainson's hawks playing hopscotch across a shifting grid of clouds. Hunting prairie falcons plunging the prairies into sudden silence.

It was spring then, too, and a wet spring, just like the spring Linda and I first set foot on the grassland together— the spring of 1989. We were working on another book, called *The Feather Quest*. It was our first project together, not counting our marriage, which was, then, not quite two years old.

"Do you remember the long-billed curlew we had here on our first trip?" I mused, nodding toward what is generously called a "pasture." "It's the only one we've ever had on the Pawnee."

Linda sighed. "That was somebody else," she said.

"No it wasn't," I proclaimed.

"Yes it was," Linda repeated, using the tonal qualities she might have employed if responding to an airline reservation menu on the phone. "Every time we come here you say, 'Do you remember the curlew?' And every time I tell you it wasn't me. And then I tell you that this isn't where we had our curlew. 'Our' curlew was farther out on the drive."

"Huh," I said. "Could have sworn I'd had a long-billed curlew only that one time on the Pawnee."

The sun was up, but the air was cold—thirty degrees on the dashboard thermometer. Frost lay thick on the carpet of buffalo grass and the lips of primroses, but only in the lower areas, where the cold air had settled. By the time we got to the crest of the hill, the atmosphere inside and outside the van had begun to thaw.

Squeedle. A horned lark called from the side of the road and lofted into the air, climbing skyward like it was bounding up invisible stairs. More and more of the rakish-looking birds—mostly singles, males—began flushing off the road. By the second week in May, most females are off incubating, and some are already tending young. Breeding season for this classic prairie species begins very early.

When we'd visited the prairie back on the second of February, there was only one bird that seemed unfazed by the frozen landscape. This was the horned lark. Over the course of our three-day trip, we tallied a meager total of seventeen bird species. They included one merlin, two ferruginous hawks, three northern flickers . . . you get the picture. The prairie, in winter, is an empty and lifeless place.

With one notable exception. Horned larks were not only present but common. They lined the roadsides. They flew in undulating waves. Their brittle call notes shivered in defiance of the white noise of the winter landscape. And while most of the horned larks that spend the winter on the Pawnee are destined to breed in the Arctic, horned larks rank among the most common breeding birds on the prairies. It has been estimated that upward of 60 percent of all the birds that breed on the shortgrass prairies are, in fact, horned larks.

"Stop!" Linda commanded.

As photographer's helper, I complied. Applied the brake and eased to a halt. But Linda's body language—left shoulder angled toward the side-view mirror, 200–400-millimeter lens pointed at a hundred-degree angle to the front of the car—told me I'd seriously overshot the subject. She settled back in her seat without taking any shots and without comment, which was comment enough.

"I thought you said 'Stop.' "

"No. I said *'Stop!'* "

"Well, it sounded like 'Stop.' What was it?"

"Horned lark," she replied. "Flew," she said.

"Oh," I observed, looking out across a landscape so sparsely vegetated it made the gravel roadbed seem lush. "Plenty more where he came from," I added as I put the car into gear. "I'd say that along this stretch horned larks are only slightly less common—"

"Stop!" Linda said again.

This time I saw her subject (and could better gauge my braking distance). A western meadowlark on a fence post marking the boundary between state and federal property and the official beginning of the Pawnee Grassland. I eased to a stop. The bird stayed put. Linda started shooting. Happy as a photographer with a subject.

Off and on through the pages of this book, you've been wooed and teased by references to meadowlarks. There are two reasons for this. First, they are common breeders in the High Plains. Second, they are wonderful. Big, plump, distinctive, vocal, and fairly genial when it comes to admirers and photographers.

Most people are surprised to learn that meadowlarks are blackbirds, falling in the same family group as cowbirds and grackles. Western meadowlark is the state bird of Kansas, Montana, Nebraska, North Dakota, Oregon, and Wyoming, making it the second most popular species among the ranks of state birds (runner-up to northern cardinal, with seven states to its credit). It has a breeding range that encompasses almost everything that might be construed as "the West," and a few places that can't—like extreme southeastern Ontario and even extreme western New York.

One of Linda's and my perennial debates has to do with eastern versus western meadowlark and which is the better singer. Eastern meadowlark's song is a slow, clear, whistled lament. Western meadowlark's song is quick, happy, rollicking. It sounds as if the bird had a song in mind, screwed up after the opening notes, and then hurried or improvised the end. Maybe partiality is a matter of what you grow up with. Maybe it depends on your mood.

When Linda settled back into the seat, her expression said, "Framed glossies on the rec-room wall."

"Okay," she said, looking down, checking her LCD screen. "We can go now," she translated, after several seconds elapsed and the van stayed put. Only then did she notice that I was busy studying the printed sign stapled to the grassland's boundary marker:

Bubonic Plague is an infectious disease whish [*sic*] once referred [*sic*] to as "The Black Death." Prairie Dogs, ground squirrels and other rodents in this area may be infected with PLAGUE. Plague may be transmitted to humans through contact with infected animals or fleas.

There followed a list of seven precautionary measures recommended by the Weld County Department of Public Health and Environment. The first one read: "Walk only on paved paths"—a difficult directive to adhere to in a place where even the roads aren't paved. Number 5 read: "Avoid Fleas."

"Huh," I said, putting the van in gear. "Let's go on and

see if we can find a paved path." We continued across the cattle guard. It wouldn't have stopped a flea anyway.

There was barbed wire fence along the south side of the road now, offering perches for Brewer's and vesper sparrows and the occasional lark bunting. A compact, triangular-winged, short-tailed sparrow (and state bird of Colorado) the lark bunting must rank just behind the horned lark as the Pawnee Grassland's most common denizen. The males are stunning. Jet-black with white shoulder patches, which, when they go aloft in their aerial displays, they flash for effect—and they go aloft often, vocalizing as they climb, vocalizing as they descend on rowing wings.

Their song is a run-on series of sequential chips, croaks, warbles, and trills, which reminds me of a throaty canary. One displaying lark bunting commonly sets off a chain reaction. My memory of twenty years ago is of the whole landscape filled with wing-rowing forms and the air ringing like the inside of a pet shop.

Now, we were running into a bird here, a bird there.

"Probably just early in the season," I suggested.

"Hope so," Linda agreed.

But the paucity of prairie dogs at the dog town on the north and south sides of the road had nothing to do with the progression of season. Prairie dogs don't migrate and they don't hibernate. The dog colony was "plagued out."

"See any of those long-tailed guinea pigs on your side?"

"Just a few," Linda observed. "Also a couple of burrowing owls way out. How about you?"

"Ditto," I said. "One dog fairly close to the road. Can you hear him?"

Of course she could. The call sounds like a cross between a chirp and a bullet ricochet. It's intended to get attention, and it does.

The danger for prairie dogs is very real, and the attention they are getting is profound. Historically, North America's prairie dogs waged a successful defensive campaign against a host of predatory species—including hawks, coyotes, and badgers—and estimates of their pre–Lewis and Clark population are absolutely mind-boggling.

Right up there with bison, prairie dogs were among the environmental engineers of the prairie. Today, as then, a whole host of prairie animals are to a varying degree dependent upon prairie dogs for the habitat dog towns provide. Animals such as prairie rattlesnake and gopher snake, burrowing owl, and swift fox all use prairie dog burrows. The federally endangered black-footed ferret's life is contingent upon prairie dogs, and the threatened mountain plover's hardly less so.

Mountain plover like dirt and places with scant vegetation. Prairie dog towns, pocked with excavations and continuously mowed by rodent teeth, are made to order. If you look at a town, the mini-volcano-like mounds that are burrow openings make the prairie landscape look like it's suffering a bad case of acne. If you study the vegetation in the town, it looks like it's been ravaged by a rotary mower with the blade set for destruct.

Therein lies the problem. Prairie dogs not only eat grass and forbs but like to keep the areas around their burrows close-cropped. It's a prairie dog's way of being both safe and tidy. Ranchers look at all that bare ground and convert it into the pounds of beef their cattle did not put on. Perhaps even more than coyotes and the federal government, ranchers hate prairie dogs. After a nearly century-long campaign to wipe them off the face of the planet (a campaign in which the Department of Agriculture was an active participant), success has caused a conflict as big as the prairies and as bitter as alkali flats. There are now so few prairie dogs in many parts of the animal's range that they have even been considered candidates for the federal threatened and endangered species list.

The Pawnee Grassland is right at the center of the debate, and Forest Service biologists are right in the cross hairs of opposing groups. On the one hand are the ranchers, who are pretty much of the traditional opinion that the only good prairie dog is a dead one.

On the other side of the mound are a host of prairie dog supporters, made up of many well-known national conservation and animal rights organizations all operating under the banner of the "Prairie Dog Coalition." Prairie dog rights remain a contentious issue. The debate eats up a great deal of the Forest Service personnel's time.

Ultimately, here on the Pawnee Grassland, biologists developed a management plan that calls for a ceiling of 8,500 prairie dogs (up from 1,000) on the 196,060 acres they control. In addition, the state of Colorado has instituted a closed season to coincide with the rodent's spring breeding season.

But these measures still do not address the more alarming and very real problem of plague. Linda and I were looking at a colony that had been decimated two years ago and was only now in the early stages of recovery. We were to come across other, larger colonies that were likewise ghost-dog towns.

"Do you want to get some shots of the owls?" I asked Linda.

She thought about it. Weighed the odds. Two owls, masters at the game of hide-and-seek with about 150 vacant holes to chose from and the power of flight, versus one five-foot, two-inch photographer burdened with about twenty-five pounds of equipment.

"We're losing good light," she said.

In case you aren't married to a photographer, I'll tell you that this means no.

Everyone's Idea of Eden

We continued on the old birding route past the old foundation on the top of the hill, down to Road 67, where, in the old Lane *Birder's Guide to Colorado*, you were directed to turn right. We went straight up the hill instead, heading toward the snowcapped peaks of the Rockies, which were glowing in the light of a beautiful spring morning.

The Pawnee Grassland is not flat. Certainly there are

level areas that someone with a restricted sense of geography might call "plains," but, unlike much of the Comanche Grassland, the Pawnee rises and falls like an ocean of painted swells. In this year of lavish snow cover and bountiful rains, the swells were also wonderfully green. Given the close-cropped nature of shortgrass prairie grasses (grasses that will scarcely reach your boot tops when fully grown), the vista before us resembled a well-groomed golf course.

If golfers dream of heaven, it looks, I suspect, much like the Pawnee Grassland. In fact, the Pawnee even comes with hazards.

There are, intruded into the rolling landscapes, occasional sharp dips. There are deeper gullies. There is, most of all, a bumper crop of prickly pears—in fact, there are large parts of the Pawnee Grassland where the label "cactusland" would be much more apt. The cactus has always been here. How much was here in historic times and whether overgrazing by cattle has caused the plant to flourish is a matter of debate. One thing is for certain, in mid-June, when the magenta-colored flowers bloom, the Pawnee Grassland becomes a subject worthy of a National Geographic Society calendar.

But we were here in May. Cameras don't have a compensation setting for a month from now.

We continued down Road 96. While birds were present, they were not overly plentiful—at least not as plentiful as memory makes them. When Linda and I had made our first trip here, we were astonished by, and wrote about, the exciting numbers of birds: lark bunting, McCown's longspur, and the beautiful and prized chestnut-collared longspur.

But over time, over the course of multiple visits, we've watched numbers slip and seen once-common birds become difficult, even impossible, to find. Chestnut-collared longspurs, once fairly common, have grown increasingly scarce. Mountain plover, once here for the scanning, now go missing after days of search.

Part of the grassland's declining bird numbers is undoubtedly related to drought. For the past six years, the Pawnee has suffered the same rain shortage as the rest of the prairies. Drought affects not only bird populations but also their willingness to breed. Furthermore, as regards mountain plover, the grasslands have had to compete for what plover there are.

I mentioned that mountain plover love dirt. You take away the prairie dogs, you take away the substrate mountain plover favor. What these plover have found is an alternative substrate. Plowed fields! There's lots of dirt there. So the birds plant their nests between the furrows, only to lose them to subsequent harrowing, disking, spraying, and other farming-related hazards.

But overall populations of mountain plover and other prairie bird species have fallen and continue to fall. According to one Pawnee Grassland biologist, the number of mountain plover actually breeding on the grassland has averaged close to zero for the past five years. This year, despite the rains, despite a great deal of active management, there were known to be two pairs. We'd be lucky to find one. And I couldn't help but think of the hundreds of birders who would be coming to the grassland in the next few weeks hoping to find their life mountain plover.

"What's that?" Linda asked, pointing.

I'll bet you think I'm going to say we found a mountain plover. Nope. Wish it were.

"I'd say it looks like a bunch of shot-up televisions and computer monitors."

And that's what it was! We had reached the turnoff to one of the area's most popular shooting ranges—one of the most popular uses in this land of multiple use. It seemed that at least some "patrons" couldn't wait to drive the extra mile into the range so they could set up their targets of opportunity along the main road.

The term "shooting range" as it relates to national grasslands is neither precise nor defining. With the exception of the Crow Valley Campground, a person can discharge a firearm anywhere on the Pawnee. But owing to topography, some places are more popular among shooters than others. Recreational shooters need a backdrop (both to stop a bullet and to prop up a target). The larger, steep-sided watersheds that snake their way through the grassland serve this function—and suffer for it, too. The range we were surveying looked like a cross between a landfill and a war zone.

I'm not going to belabor this. I'm not going to point a castigating finger at gun owners and use the abuse of a natural area to lobby for a gun-free America.

For the record, I own firearms. For the record, I belong to a National Rifle Association–affiliated shooting range, which I use regularly. But when I go shooting, I collect and take away my used targets and my backdrop. I collect my spent brass and empty ammunition boxes. I try to leave the range better than I found it (just like all target shooters in America will swear they do).

Why anyone would think it is acceptable (much less safe) to haul unwanted appliances to a natural area and shoot them into shard with firearms is beyond my comprehension.

"Some guys even drove a pickup truck in here and shot it to pieces," a man who was collecting spent brass cartridges confided to me. "They hit everything but the battery. Missed it clean. I got five dollars for it."

He was also getting a buck thirty a pound for the brass he collected. He said he scavenged two and a half tons last year.

Okay. So it's an ill wind that doesn't blow somebody some good. And maybe it's a good thing that shooting, for the most part, is concentrated in a few areas (even if these tend to be areas where there are seasonal, environmentally sensitive watercourses). But unregulated shooting, by uncaring individuals, is just one more headache for the people who manage our grasslands to contend with.

And it reflects badly upon responsible sportsmen and target shooters.

And it's one more sign of grasslands under pressure.

Speaking of signs . . .

"You don't suppose that the morons who shoot up television sets are related to the people who shoot roadside signs, do you?" I asked.

"Probably," Linda agreed. "Same genus, different species. Probably fall into the same class as people who spray-paint graffiti on water tanks and Forest Service signs."

Did I mention that the Forest Service has a vandalism problem, too? Well, it does.

"We're losing light," Linda said, again.

TURNAROUND IS JUST OVER THE HILL

It's tough coming to a place you love and finding it diminished, but that's what we were experiencing. Twenty years of change; twenty years of increased "multiple use" versus twenty-twenty memories. It's not that the Pawnee's magic is gone. Almost two hundred thousand acres of pure prairie magic is hard to undermine. But the signs of change were there.

From the seasonal road closings (necessary to protect nesting birds), to the testiness of landowners, to the sheriff department's drive-through of the Crow Valley Campground, to the supersize, spray-painted message across a water-holding tank beside the road that read: "REPUBLICANS ARE HUMAN."

It has been aptly stated that there is no such thing as a "wildlife problem." There are only people problems. And in many different ways, people are bringing their problems—even if they frame them as "ambitions," "hobbies," "rights," or "interests"—to the grasslands.

This is what I was thinking as we topped a rise and I

took in a view that included the old ranch house I remembered and the several small, newly built residential homes and the big microwave relay tower that I did not; and Linda said, "stop."

It wasn't "Stop," which means come to a halt.

It wasn't *"Stop!"* which means *brake now!*

It was simply "stop." This means: ohmygod; don't move a muscle; don't breathe; just ease-to-a-stop-please-please-please-as-soon-as-you-can-and-pray-pray-pray-it-doesn't-leave.

On my side of the car, about eye level and forty feet away, was a swift fox looking through my window. It was sunning itself by the entrance to its den. It was appraising us with cool detachment.

From where I sat, it was beautiful. From behind the viewfinder of Linda's camera, it must have been glorious.

"That was awesome," the photographer said about four hundred frames later. Flashing a prairie-size grin, reaching over, and giving my knee a squeeze.

Yes, the Pawnee still has the power to captivate. Even gratify.

Of Longspurs and Plover
and How and Where to Find 'Em

We turned east onto Road 104 after passing the old one-room schoolhouse—one of the few prairie schools left standing. We knew this stretch of road. Knew it well.

"Pull off when we get past the cattle guard?" Linda inquired more than said.

"Right," I confirmed more than agreed. "Still have any memory left in that thing?" I teased, gesturing toward the camera in her hands.

"Plenty," she assured, grabbing and shaking a box of unused memory cards in my direction. "Bring on the natural wonders."

We found some. But we also knew how and where to look. And did I mention that Linda and I are very lucky?

Just past the place where the fence juts toward the road, across from the pastures where mountain plover used to breed, a small black-and-chestnut-colored bird sprang into the air and landed on the other side of the road.

"Chestnutcollaredlongspur!" we shouted in unison and in harmony. A prairie specialty, a pearl of great price.

It was a sad, sad day for McCown's longspurs when the folks up in R & D wheeled out their new chestnut-collared model. McCown's, the shortgrass longspur, is dapper enough. Breeding males are mostly gray with whitish faces, black breasts, and a touch of rust on the shoulder. When they go aloft, which they do often, the white tail is embossed with a distinctive T pattern. Females are similarly but more subtly patterned.

But the chestnut-collared longspur is a designer bird. Favoring midgrass prairie, breeding males seem cast from elemental earth with darkish backs, blackish bellies, chestnut napes, and ocher-colored faces. They look like birds on the warpath. They look too stunning for words.

And if you can manage to get close enough, if you catch

them in the right light, if you have a pure heart, you'll discover something not even mentioned in field guides. The lower bellies of males are not black. They're maroon!

The stretch of road we were on has always held chestnut-collareds. We were counting on it now, and we were not disappointed. We found four pairs. Paired but still in the early stages of courtship. When they flushed, they didn't fly far. When the males went aloft, they gave forth a flight song reminiscent of a western meadowlark's song but higher pitched.

It was while following one of these displaying adults back to earth that my binoculars picked up the form of a mountain plover way out on a grass-poor stretch of plain. A single bird, pale as winter grass, silent as the heat waves that rippled between us.

It was feeding but watching us. Standing in the haughty manner of mountain plover, stalking in the halting manner of its kind—a bird with a fawn-colored back, a cream-colored breast, and an expression so baleful a basset hound might die from envy.

"How did you find that?" Linda said, picking up her camera, heading off in the direction of the plover, not waiting for an answer. If the chestnut-collareds were stunned by the sudden shift in focus, they didn't show it. In fact, they probably welcomed the diversion.

Birders in general, and photographers in particular, are sometimes guilty of overzealous appreciation. Both interactions prompt practitioners to force intimacy with the objects of their attention—often to the point that birds fly, putting distance between themselves and their admirers.

Under normal circumstances, evasion hardly constitutes a disruption. Flight is just how birds deal with problems. Something threatens or annoys them, they fly away. But in the case of birds that are highly desirable (like mountain plover), or birds that are breeding and whose mobility has been compromised, compounded harassment can be both disruptive and even harmful. While the impact of birders and photographers is less than many other stresses, it is not inconsequential—and it is just one more pressure on grasslands and grassland species.

So I was impressed by the way Linda approached her subject, the mountain plover. She took her time. She gave the bird the opportunity to get used to her presence and to assess that the threat she posed was minimal. She never pushed it to the point of flight. She walked away with the bird—probably a male, in its large territory—still feeding. The female, incubating her clutch of four eggs, was clearly someplace else.

"That was great," Linda assessed. If she was beaming after her encounter with the fox, she was glowing now.

We weren't losing light anymore; it was already lost, and while photography has much to do with subjects, it has everything to do with good light. By 10:00 A.M. the glare is too harsh, the shadows too disfiguring for quality shots, and bird activity, even at the height of the breeding season, tapers off.

I had notes to commit to the computer. Linda had a "gazillion" shots to edit. There might even be time, later, for a little birding in Crow Valley; we could see what kinds of migrants the trees had seduced from the sky.

On the way back, we stopped for a particularly photogenic thirteen-lined ground squirrel. A little farther on, I took up the challenge presented by a group of five male pronghorn south of the road, who indicated (by signs indecipherable to anyone without a Y chromosome) that they wanted to drag.

At forty miles per hour, with the antelope still half an antelope's length ahead of Piggy's front bumper, we called it a draw. I backed off on the accelerator; the antelope quartered off to the south and slackened their pace.

"Literature says they can do forty-five," I said to Linda, who just shook her head.

Can you guess which way? If you don't have a Y chromosome, I'll bet you can.

Evening Primrose

May 17 and foggy. We were leaving the Pawnee, heading north toward the South Dakota Badlands, hoping to catch up with the season.

It was our fault, of course. We'd dawdled. Found too much to see and do in the Pawnee, coming finally to the realization that the young foxes in their dens would have to mature without us and that the prickly pear would bloom but we couldn't be here to see it.

That's the problem with spring, its glory, too. It's fleeting. By the time you catch the pulse of it, it's passed you by. By the time you have seen enough springs to know this, your life has known more springs to recall than there are springs yet to experience.

We turned out of Crow Valley with windows down, to savor the songs of all the breeding birds that had arrived. With regrets, we passed the turnoff for the tour route.

"Be neat to get some shots of longspurs in the fog," Linda coaxed.

"Would be," I agreed, driving on.

She didn't press; I didn't relent. We'd experienced a great deal already. But you could spend a lifetime and never see it all. Nature offers no guarantees. Only surprises. Gifts. Like the one that greeted us now. A farewell present from the Pawnee.

By the time I was conscious of the mass of white blossoms smothering the landscape, I realized that I'd been aware for some time. They flanked the roadside. To the east and north they went on to the foggy horizon, so possibly forever (there was no way of knowing for certain), a veil of snow-colored blossoms that had transformed the prairie overnight.

It looked as though the Milky Way had settled onto the land, or a million silver-shod pixies had danced atop the grass, leaving petaled imprints where they trod.

Only once before in my life have I seen a landscape so magically transformed. It was in Kenya. I was leading a tour. Driving through the grassland north of Nairobi. Suddenly, we realized that millions of tiny white butterflies were moving across the highway, about a foot above the road, and quickly deduced that our scope was much too limited. The entire countryside, from horizon to horizon, was awash in a sea of butterflies, all single-mindedly moving in the same direction. Like the flowers, they turned the green landscape white.

I pulled onto a side road and stopped the van.

"This is incredible," I whispered.

"Primrose," Linda breathed. "I've never seen them like this before, have you?"

I had not. Not in my trips, not in my dreams. We'd found our first evening primrose blooming back in April in the Comanche Grassland. A flower the color of Chinese porcelain and the texture of tissue paper. Big and showy, composed of four perfect heart-shaped petals attached to a single stalk.

Evening primrose looks entirely too fine and delicate to cut it in the prairie environment—a place where only the toughest flowers survive. But looks are deceiving, and the primroses, like the other flowers that flourish in the prairie environment, have special modifications that make them contenders in the open prairie arena.

First, while the flower itself seems gossamer fine, the stem is short, fibrous, and tough—a good wind-resistant combination. The leaves are narrow and small—reducing the amount of surface area subject to evaporation—and they are covered by short hairs to trap moisture and diminish the desiccating effects of the wind. Often, too, the flowers sprout in bare earth, away from other plants and grasses that might compete for the moisture trapped in the soil; and they bloom early, from April to June, to take advantage of what water is available, whether from winter snows or from spring rains.

But the desiccation-defeating characteristic that gives the primrose not only its competitive edge but its name is the flower's habit of blooming in the evening, after the sun has lost its strength. This is how we found them, the morning after. A bounty of evening primroses that had responded to the season's lavish rains by blooming in unprecedented numbers.

We minced our way through blossoms so as not to mar their perfection, and to avoid the prickly pear that flourished around them. Like magic, like justice, the carpet of blossoms was not evenly distributed. There were areas where blossoms dominated, a carpet fit for a coronation or a bride. There were other places where the blossoms were more spare—one or two here, several there. If you looked closely, it seemed that where the stands of prickly pear grew thickest, the flowers grew elsewhere.

I'm sure there's a lesson here. Maybe even a fable. I'll leave the crafting to you.

Overhead, the pixielike tinkling of horned larks mixed with the fairylike giggling of McCown's longspurs. Above them the sound of some high-flying commuter jet fell to earth, oblivious to the magic that had transformed the earth, if only for a little time, because primroses have one more death-defeating adaptation.

They bloom for a brief time. In a few short days, the blossoms turn pink, then wither. Quicker than spring, they cheat a lingering death by embracing a swift one.

Years ago I read a book called *The Dirty Dozen*, just one among many books spawned by World War II that fell, in its literary value, somewhere between *From Here to Eternity* and the Sgt. Rock comic books kids my age squandered their dimes on (instead of spending fifteen cents on the Classic Comics we told our moms we were buying). It's been my experience that few books are devoid of some redeemable element tucked between their covers, and this book was no exception.

There was a line, attributed to an English pub owner's daughter, who was attracted to the book's main character, a troubleshooting major (played by Lee Marvin in the movie). Said this smitten young lass, in the spring of her youth: "It's not spring until you can plant your foot upon a dozen flowers."

She might have said "daisies." It hardly matters.

I relate this because that observation occurred to me as I stood amid that ocean of primroses—each and every one perfect in its beauty and symmetry; each and every one destined to die—and I wondered . . .

Just when is spring? At what point in the timeline between winter and summer does this season really happen?

Is spring just a series of run-on events? Or is there a threshold? A crossing point? A standard of measure? Like being able to plant your foot upon a dozen flowers!

I searched around and spotted a cluster of blossoms that looked like it might pass the test. I glanced over to make sure Linda wasn't looking.

Walking over, I selected a place where all the magic of spring seemed to have pooled. There, on open prairie, were flowers crowding flowers, each and every one a perfect heart quartet arrayed around a spray of golden filaments that burst from the center like a bouquet of sparks.

I raised my size-thirteen (not twelve to fourteen, thirteen!) shoes and sighted along my shin, making sure of my aim. It had to be right the first time. There is no second chance with spring.

A little to the right, I thought. Make sure you include that big saucy one, there.

Now, a little down, I corrected. That one under your toe is past its prime. There! Perfect.

Overhead, the horned larks held their breath. The longspurs hovered with sheathed beaks. I lowered my foot until it was level with the tops of the flowers, until I could feel the strength of the season pushing back against my sole, and tried to estimate how many blossoms were blocked from view (without losing my balance). I came up with . . .

About a dozen.

You thought I was going to step on them, didn't you? Silly you. Only a barbarian would trample on the flowers that constitute the gold standard for spring. Multiple use might cover a lot of things, but acts of barbarism it does not.

Since I was in an estimating mood, I thought I'd try to calculate how many primroses stood in front of me. Using an average of 350 blossoms per 100 square feet, figuring that to the far hilltop I was looking at an area about three quarters of a square mile, I came up with approximately 73,180,800 flowers.

While that figure represents a prodigious amount of work on the part of a small dance troupe of pixies, it falls far short of the numeric mass of the Milky Way.

But, you might be thinking, your estimate covered only the area in front of you. What about the area behind you?

Sorry. The figure remains the same. Behind us there was nothing but a flowerless field of winter wheat—as static as it was green. The gift of primroses fell only on the prairies. No less than you would expect.

CHAPTER 10

Custer State Park, South Dakota

The herd's matriarch, now about forty feet away, gave us about three seconds' appraisal, then continued on, her cinnamon-colored yearling right on her heels. The Road Pig outweighed her by about ninety-seven hundred pounds (even a large male buffalo doesn't tip the scales much over two thousand pounds), but bison in Custer State Park are pretty used to automobiles, and even some of the idiots who drive them.

There has been only one bison-related fatality in the park, and while injuries are not annual, "incidents" are. The plodding manner of bison, coupled with the mercifully scant number of signs urging people to respect the animals, lulls many tourists into a false sense of complacency. Through the viewing screens of their digital cameras they may not note the danger signs (raised tail, defecation) and may even ignore the last stage of a challenge, which is the animal's focused approach.

The next stage is called a "charge," and since bison can attain speeds of thirty miles per hour (about the speed of a Thoroughbred horse), dawdling to get a great shot when an animal the size of a Dumpster is trying to run you over can be a costly mistake.

"Close enough?" I shouted back to Linda, who was in the process of climbing onto the roof of the RV "for a better angle."

"The light stinks!" she shouted back.

In case you are not married to a photographer, this means the proximity was fine.

It was more than fine, and in about thirty seconds it went from fine to great to spectacular to unbelievable, as about 150 American bison ambled past our vehicle so close you could see the Road Pig reflected in their eyes, smell the little bluestem on their breath, and hear the crunch as the animals reduced bite-size chunks of prairie to fodder. When one of the animals began to use the front end of our RV as a rubbing post, it struck me that I was as close to the "Lords of the Prairies" as anyone is entitled to get.

Given the fact that in 1890 there were probably fewer than a thousand plains bison left on Earth, this is a very big entitlement.

The policy of South Dakota's Custer State Park is that their enclosed seventy thousand acres belongs to wildlife, especially the eight hundred to fourteen hundred free-ranging bison that the park is famous for. But before Europeans reached the New World, the American bison's playground was considerably larger, ranging from the Bering Sea to Central Mexico and encompassing virtually all of western Canada and almost all of the United States—extending as far east as western New York, eastern Pennsylvania, central Virginia, the central Carolinas, and Georgia.

But the very core of the animal's range, and where most of the estimated 30 to 40 million bison were found, was the prairies. Not even the plains of Africa has ever sustained a population of grazing animals this immense, the dependence upon after-the-fact estimates of the bison population notwithstanding. Most of those who actually saw the herds before they were eradicated were too humble or impressed to ascribe a number to them.

While a small percentage of bison were resident, most were migratory. They traveled annually across the open grasslands, moving generally east in the spring to take advantage of the nutritional riches of the tallgrass prairies, retreating west in the fall. In their wake, the hungry herds left a changed environment. Thirty to 40 million grazing animals are not just an ecological component, they are a force of nature!

Lack of rainfall gives rise to the kingdom of grass. Fire

protects its integrity and defends its borders. But fire had an ally. This was the bison. Browsing animals, designed to clip and digest the silica-reinforced blades that are grass.

Unlike cattle, bison more or less eat on the run, grabbing mouthfuls of grass and forbs as they amble along. More bison mean more mouthfuls, and explorers spoke of finding areas grazed and trampled to bare earth in the wake of large herds. From an ecological standpoint, even this is not necessarily a bad thing. For the most part, foraging bison pruned and shaped, rather than denuded, the prairie landscape, browsing a little more here, a little less there. The result was a rich vegetative mosaic, with grasses and forbs found in various stages of regeneration in the wake of herds—some plants recovering rapidly, some more slowly, benefiting a range of prairie birds and animals.

Where grasses were heavily grazed and the earth torn up by tens of thousands of feet, dirt-loving horned larks colonized. A little more standing vegetation, and McCown's longspurs felt right at home. More lightly grazed grasslands might be home to the taller-grass-favoring chestnut-collared longspurs or perhaps upland sandpipers. The tallest, richest grasslands, revitalized and recovered from last year's grazing, would now be perfect for bobolinks or Baird's and grasshopper sparrows.

Bison were not just part of the prairie. They were a key component of the ecological dynamic that was the prairie. If the prairies had been left intact but the bison removed, they would be different prairies today in terms of the plants and animals that would thrive there.

But the prairies were not left intact. And the bison were removed, too. Slaughtered actually.

It took about two hundred years of European colonization for North America's largest land animal to be eliminated east of the Mississippi (two animals killed in Wisconsin in 1832 might have been the last). It took about half a century more to eradicate most of the rest. Beginning in the late 1700s, a market was developing for buffalo hides. As westward expansion, aided by the railroad, made deeper inroads into the heart of the prairies and the bison's domain, the rate of slaughter accelerated.

By 1870, equipped with powerful, accurate, fast-loading, breechloading rifles, buffalo hunters were killing an estimated 2.5 million mature animals a year, resulting in, in the words of Paul Johnsgard, professor emeritus of biology at the University of Nebraska, "perhaps the greatest mass killing of large animals in history." A killing spree that went on for over a decade.

At first appraisal, the annual removal of 2.5 million individual animals from a herd of no fewer than 30 million animals might not seem insupportable. But this figure fails to include the number of animals that were being taken by native people, nor does it take into account the impact of natural predation or attrition relating to accident and disease.

In addition, the greatest impact of market gunning was upon adult animals, the core breeders, and since there was no such thing as a closed season on bison, the killing of females in the spring left their calves to die of neglect—a biological double whammy. Just when the bison population's attrition was going up, new recruitment into their ranks was going down.

The results speak for themselves. By 1883, North America's last major herd of ten thousand bison was eliminated in the Black Hills of South Dakota. Three years later, in 1886, W. T. Hornaday, the chief taxidermist for the National Museum, spent several months near Miles City, Montana, trying to secure specimens for a planned exhibition. He collected, after considerable effort, twenty-six animals, but this experience convinced the future founder of the American Bison Society that the animals faced extinction.

Fortunately, several farsighted individuals had already come to the same conclusion and had begun independent captive-rearing programs, using primarily captured calves. Among these propagation pioneers was Frederick Dupree of Fort Pierre, South Dakota, who in 1883 began raising bison using, as a core, nine orphaned calves. In 1901, after Dupree's death, the rancher Scotty Phillips purchased the eighty-three head, which, under his care, had increased to about five hundred animals by 1918. These are the animals that were the foundation of the Custer State Park herd. Some of their descendants were around Linda and me now.

A WORLD WITHOUT

Linda was right. The light was stinky. It was only an hour after sunrise, and while the sky was, as promised, "mostly clear," the sun had elected to park itself behind that section of sky that was mostly not.

This is not to say that this Sunday morning, on the edge of South Dakota's famed Black Hills, lacked for charm. In fact, it was beautiful.

The Black Hills are an orphaned extension of the Rockies, formed 60 million years ago by the same geologic spasm that was thrusting up the great future tourist meccas of Colorado, Wyoming, and Montana. The overlying limestone and upthrusting granite were shaped over thousands of years into the photogenic spires and domes tourists frame in their digital cameras today. As the ice receded at the close of the most recent glacial period, the landscape became carpeted by forests, first of spruce, later of pine. When the region entered a warmer and drier era, about eight thousand years ago, and much of it surrendered to grass, the forests of the Paha Sapa of the Lakota Sioux, literally the "Hills of Black," endured.

An island of trees in a sea of grass.

George Armstrong Custer, two years before blundering into eternal fame, led a scientific expedition here in 1874. When he wasn't roughriding or trustbusting, Teddy Roosevelt played here. Presidents Coolidge, in 1927, and Dwight David Eisenhower, in 1953, retreated here, too. And every year, hundreds of thousands of Americans visit the Black Hills, savoring not only the scenic beauty but also some of the region's principal natural and man-made attractions. Wind Cave National Park, adjacent to Custer

State Park and home to a subterranean marvel, is one. Mount Rushmore, whose presidential likenesses are cut into the 60-million-year-old bedrock of the Black Hills, is another.

But many people come, if not expressly or exclusively, to see the bison herds in Custer and Wind Cave. For this reason, the grassy plains and tongues of prairie licking into the forested hills must rank among the most visited grasslands in North America.

Not that you would have known that this morning. Linda and I were the only visitors in sight—had been for half an hour now. And this was the park's "open house" weekend. No fees. Two days of programs and events. It was the kickoff to the summer tourist season, and spring was bursting at the seams.

Managing the Herd

The bison were mostly across the road now. Heading for one of the "supplemental mineral licks" that are part of the park's management plan (and that seem to be located at points where the free-ranging bison may be easily viewed from roadside pullouts). A couple of mature bulls, the herd's traditional caboose, were bringing up the rear. Big guys. Way up there in the two-thousand-pound class. Heavy in the shoulders, lean in the hips. Either one of them could have served as the model on an old nickel.

American bison are remarkable animals. Descended from ancestral stock originating in Siberia, honed to a symbiotic edge with and by the prairies, they are, in many respects, just big, shaggy cattle. They graze. They herd. They have a social structure.

They can even interbreed! The bison herd in Custer State Park carries, in its genetic makeup, a bit of bovine bolstering that renders them not quite "genetically pure" and is one of the reasons that the Custer herd and the 350 or so thoroughbred bison that reside on the adjacent Wind Cave National Park are separated by fences (and a mile-wide buffer during the summer breeding season).

But the ancestral stock for today's Hereford, Angus, and Holstein cattle came from Asia, a wet environment. Bison hail from a corner of the planet that is cold and dry. As a result, their water needs are several times less than those of cattle, making them more perfect grazers for arid grasslands.

One thing they are not is beautiful. Big? Yes. Rugged? No question. Environmentally attuned? Absolutely. Impressive? You bet. Beautiful? Not a chance.

A buffalo (American for bison) is a front-heavy ungulate with a head too large and hips too small to win any ribbons at the local county fair stock show. Even bison calves skirt the "oh, it's so cute" label that we affix to most young animals. In a crowd of young heifers, a bison calf would stand out like the class thug in the school choir.

The color of adult bison is blah to blackish brown. The woolly pelage is tough, fibrous, matted about the head and shoulders, and begs a currycomb. The more sparsely haired hindquarters make the animals appear half flayed. Now, in spring, with their winter coats coming off in chunks, the animals looked particularly disheveled. At all times of year, and at every opportunity, the entire unit is treated to a self-anointed coat of dust.

The animals' dark eyes hesitate between bovine simplicity and dull cunning. Their horns, which are not just there for show, are symmetrically curled on males and turn up at the tips on females.

This is not the only difference between males and females. In addition to larger size, males have larger humps, longer beards, and woollier front legs (which make the animals look as though they were wearing pompons).

No, they are not beautiful. But they are impressive, and not only do they stop traffic but they attract it. During our travels, when we mentioned bison and where to see them in their prairie habitat, one name came up over and over again. This was Custer State Park.

Other places, including nearby Wind Cave, and Yellowstone, received honorable mention. There are now perhaps 350,000 bison in North America, most of which reside in privately owned herds (including those on native lands). But Custer is where the buffalo roam. If you want a glimpse of what the prairies used to look like, before Lewis and Clark went wandering, this is the place to go.

If you don't want to have this nostalgic image diminished by some underlying management realities, just skip the next section and move on to the rest of the book. Like the prairies themselves, like the world we have fashioned, the bison in Custer might be wild and free ranging, but they fall short of being natural.

Fifteen hundred bison don't sound like a lot compared with the tens of millions of animals that once roamed the American prairies, and therein lies the operative word: *roamed.* Before the prairie environment was turned, literally, upside down, these nomadic ungulates had about 1.2 million square miles of pasture to browse. When the grass played out over here, the animals moved over there, on to greener pastures, while the grazed areas were left to recover, naturally. The herds and the grasslands maintained this dynamic balance for thousands of years.

In the geographically limited, fence-enclosed confines of the park, this is not the case. If the grasslands become overgrazed, the animals can go as far as the fence. Then they are stuck. Their world, like their resources, is finite. The only thing they can do is turn around and go back over the same grazed terrain. It's not good from the standpoint of meeting the energetic needs of bison; it's not good for the grass.

If bison populations were static, and if available grasslands were sufficient to meet their needs (that is, if the browsers and browse were in a state of equilibrium), there wouldn't necessarily be a problem. But nature is never static. Animals have this compelling need to replicate themselves, so populations tend to increase. Grasslands are not static, either. Their productivity is closely linked to rainfall, so in times of drought they are less productive.

Nature will always strive to strike a balance between supply and demand. The nomadic feeding habit of bison is a prime example of a biological righting mechanism. But another righting mechanism in nature's operations manual is predation. Whereas procreation brings populations up, predation brings them down. In the natural prairie environment, there were not only wolves and plains grizzlies that helped maintain the natural balance, but also over one hundred thousand native hunters, whose job it was to provide for a people that virtually subsisted on bison. It has been estimated that the average prairie tribesman consumed about eight bison per year. In pre-Columbian America there were, perhaps, several hundred thousand native people on the prairies whose dietary mainstay was bison.

This comes to a lot of bison, and, in conjunction with accidents and other natural causes of death (including animal predation), this culling by native peoples helped maintain the size of North America's bison herd at a self-sustaining level.

There are no native hunters now in Custer State Park, nor are there wolves or grizzly bears. And although in 1914 two dozen bison were introduced into the park, by the late 1940s this number had grown to between twenty-five hundred and three thousand bison plus an equal number of elk (which were also reintroduced), along with reintroduced pronghorn and a bunch of feral burros whose ancestors once hauled visitors to the top of Harney Peak.

All of these animals are grazers, and Custer's grassland became severely overgrazed. There were two alternatives. Knock down the fence and let the animals roam, or reduce and control the numbers of animals. The latter course was eminently more feasible, first because there was no place for the surplus animals to go (Wind Cave had its own over-population problem), and second because not only is wild-life management feasible, but it can also be profitable.

Today, in Custer, there is an established ceiling of 968 wintering bison, if grazing conditions are optimal. Because of a prolonged drought, and its impact upon the quality of the park's grasslands, this figure has been reduced to 815, where it will remain until weather (and grass) conditions change.

To maintain this target figure, the park holds two auctions per year—one closed bid and one online—for the sale of mostly one-year-old animals. In addition, there are two hunts—one for trophy animals ("over the hill bulls") and one for nontrophy animals. The cost of a hunting tag is five thousand dollars. Profits from the sale of bison, in addition to a timber harvest and visitor revenue, have helped make the park almost self-sustaining.

How many parks can claim that?

Every October there is a bison roundup. Calves are branded and inoculated. Animals designated for auction are culled. The hunts run from October through November, after the tourist season. Wind Cave National Park has a similar roundup, but, in accordance with federal mandates, the animals cannot be sold. They are, instead, apportioned to other federal lands, including native lands.

The question you might fairly ask is how does raising bison on Custer State Park differ from raising cattle on adjacent ranchlands? I don't know. Ask a rancher.

The other question you might ask is How does the experience of driving the wildlife loop at Custer differ from, say, going to some wild animal park? Here, at least, I think I have an answer.

I think that at Custer, and in other places where North America's wildlife is managed and showcased, the ambition is to offer visitors a taste of their natural heritage—all that is left of the inexhaustible riches that once were ours (and proved not to be inexhaustible). Animal parks are trying to make something unnatural, like zebra in Virginia, appear natural.

I know that the people whose job it is to protect, preserve, and promote the riches of natural areas strive to manage the land and its animals in a way that is as close to nature as limiting realities provide. I only hope that visitors see and believe this, too. Speaking of which . . .

AFTER THE PANCAKE BREAKFAST AND THIS SIDE OF
THE BUFFALO BURGER LUNCH SPECIAL
It was almost nine o'clock now, and a few other park visitors were finally on the prowl. There is nothing quite like 150

bison to bring cars to a standstill (and they don't necessarily need to be standing in the road). Fact is, people get a thrill out of seeing these animals that they have heard so much about and whose existence is inextricably wrapped up in the national and international love affair we have with the American West.

I sometimes wonder how many people give the prairie on which that love object stands a first, much less second, thought.

And I'm sure that most viewers, seeing buffalo for the first time, look past and over and around the little things that make the experience not quite natural. The numbered red tags on the ears, the brands on the flanks, the leather radio collars worn by some individuals.

Few, I'm sure, even recognize that the animals' complacence is not exactly natural, either. If these were "wild" bison and this were three hundred years ago, you could bet that any ad hoc appearance of the animal's principal predator would have prompted a stampede worthy of a Hollywood movie.

Or haven't you seen that painting of Native Americans on hands and knees and in wolves' clothing stalking a herd of bison? Can you imagine how suspicious bison must have been of humans if a wolf disguise constituted an advantage?

The animals were more than one hundred yards away now. Most of the occupants in the cars that had stopped were augmenting their wildlife experience with digital cameras, not binoculars. The tags and collars wouldn't show.

They knew little or nothing about the park's management plan or practices. The bison scattered across the grassy landscape looked as natural as natural can be in this day and age. The smiles on the faces of the children in the cars and the approving acclaim on the faces of adults, at least, were real.

And natural.

CHAPTER 11

The Little Bighorn Battlefield, Montana

CLASH OF SEASONS

"A strong spring storm system will shift across eastern Montana and northern Wyoming . . .

"Snow can be expected in the Bighorn Mountains with accumulations of eighteen inches possible before . . .

"In lower elevations, widespread rainfall between one and two inches will cause . . .

"A flood watch is in effect for . . ."

Having gotten more than the general idea, I turned the weather band radio off.

"Haven't we heard this forecast before?" I asked the moribund form seated next to me.

"Sounds pretty nasty," Linda agreed. The precipitation being moved around by windshield wipers set on max supported this determination, as did the rain-grayed grass-scape spreading out on both sides of I-90. The car's compass indicated that we were heading north (in defiance of the east-west designation of even-numbered highways). The thermometer read thirty-nine degrees Fahrenheit. Pretty cold for May 22, but by no means unheard of in these parts. Spring weather in the northern prairies swings like the tide of battle. May is an iffy month, perhaps the iffiest month, and almost every Montana resident has memories of snow falling on Memorial Day weekend. Some even recall snow on the Fourth of July!

Memorial Day, by the way, is the day set aside for the nation to honor its war dead. It has become the unofficial kickoff to the summer vacation season, and the Mother of All Yard Sales, but this was not its intent. Having its origin in the aftermath of the Civil War, the date established by Congress in 1971, the purpose was to set aside a day for a grateful nation to pay tribute to those whose lives were sacrificed in its defense. Linda and I were heading for a battlefield where some of those lives were lost. One hundred and thirty-one years ago, the fate of a people, a culture, and an ecosystem hung in the balance here.

They triumphed. Briefly. And the 765 acres that constitute the Little Bighorn Battlefield National Monument pay lasting tribute. Much of the prairie that entombs the remains of the U.S. cavalrymen and mostly Sioux warriors who fought and died here has never been plowed, and it has not been grazed since 1891. The richness of the prairie there, now magnified by spring, attests to it.

"Look at all the flowers," I exclaimed, taking my attention off the road, surrendering to the eye-grabbing patch of purple that pretty nearly mantled the steep, north-facing slope of a roadside ridge.

"Lupine," Linda diagnosed. "Big, spiky clusters," she explained. "Grows in patches. There's some more."

Lots more. The Montana hillsides were fairly awash in flowers. Some scattered like random thoughts, some gathered in blankets as though planted by design. It had been, and continued to be, a wet spring across the prairies, and now, on the eve of Memorial Day weekend, it was late spring, too. Wildflowers are an integral part of the prairie landscape from April through October. While flowers may not dominate the landscape (this is the kingdom of grass, after all), they do enrich and enliven it, conferring upon the prairies a kaleidoscope quality that changes as early-blooming species surrender to later-blooming plants. If you cared to make the point that the purpose of grass is to serve as a backdrop to the multitude of prairie wildflowers, I wouldn't argue against it.

Not today, anyway. Not with the weight of evidence spreading out on all sides, standing out and up against the wind and the rain.

The stuff hitting the windshield sounded suddenly harder. I glanced at the thermometer and noted that the temperature had fallen another degree, and, as I watched, it dropped, again, down to thirty-seven degrees Fahrenheit . . . then thirty-six. The wet fusillade didn't diminish, but it did change in pitch again, going from *ping* to *plop*. The drops no longer spread when they spattered. Instead they sort of smushed against the glass, waiting for the wiper blade to sweep them aside.

"It's snowing," Linda announced, none too happily.

"Prairie spring," I chanted, making light of the conditions. "It's what we came out here to see. Hey, what's that patch of yellow flowers over there?" I directed.

"Some kind of yellow composite," Linda intoned. "Yellow composite" is the botanical equivalent of shrugging your shoulders. There are lots of yellow composites, many maddeningly similar.

The thermometer read thirty-five degrees now. Then it went back up to thirty-six. Then back down to thirty-five.

Amazing. Here it was almost Memorial Day weekend, and winter and spring were still duking it out. And while the flowers on both sides of the highway said summer, the snow slopping up the windshield and the thermometer said otherwise.

Thirty-four degrees . . . then, thirty-three!

"How far to the battlefield?" I asked, suddenly aware that worsening road conditions might force a change of strategy—like going on the defensive and pulling off the highway at the nearest RV park.

"About twenty miles," Linda assessed. "As the crow flies," she added.

"That's pretty funny," I observed.

"Why?" she asked.

"Because we're heading for the Crow Indian Reservation," I said.

There was silence for a time. While the highway dipped and climbed. While the prairie landscape rose and fell. As the precipitation went from snow to sleet to rain and back to sleet.

"I thought Custer fought the Sioux," Linda said.

"He did. And the Cheyenne and Arapaho. The Crow were the enemies of the Sioux. Custer used them for scouts."

"But the Sioux won," Linda asserted.

I looked out at the prairie stretching away on both sides of the van, a prairie that extended as far as eyes can see.

"Only the battle," I said. In the clash of peoples, cultures, and ethos, the prairie Indians lost the war. Somebody else got the land.

And I didn't mean the Crow Nation.

The thermometer went back up to thirty-six degrees, then thirty-seven. It was raining hard when we crossed the Little Bighorn. The river was turbulent and murky.

GONE WITH THE WIND

There are no seats or benches at the "Last Stand" monument overlooking the cluster of marble markers that stand where Custer, and the last of his command, fell. It's curious, actually, because this is a place that invites contemplation, and the view overlooking the valley beyond, the Little Bighorn below, and the site of one of the world's most studied and argued battles, is incomparable.

Particularly this morning! After a day and a night of cleansing rain. With light winds coming out of the north, a sky so blue it hurt your eyes, and a world so full of spring it fairly squeezed the other seasons off the calendar.

It was early, just after eight o'clock; opening time. Visitors, so far, were few. But park service maintenance crew members were out in force, policing the ground. Memorial Day weekend was close at hand. It's a big event for national cemeteries, and they try to look their best for residents and visitors alike.

Over the sound of leaf blowers moving grass clippings around and the guy on the ATV spraying herbicide along the tour road, I could just make out the songs of western meadowlark, vesper sparrow, and western kingbird drifting up from the grassland below. It wasn't until they turned off the leaf blowers that I detected the frail, insectlike buzz of grasshopper sparrow.

These birds would have been here, too, in late June, during the battle. First, because they are common summer residents on the mixed-grass prairies and, second, because, unlike most of the American prairies, the habitat here is little changed. A photo taken in 1879, three years after the battle, shows the same open grassland that visitors enjoy today. It extends from the hilltop-dimpled ridgeline that served as the final retreat for the besieged cavalry troops down through many gulches and vales to the river below. It's not great terrain for mounted cavalry to maneuver and a harder place for impromptu infantry to defend. Custer and his men were the first to reach this conclusion.

The old photo shows fewer trees along the river than I

could see now. It also doesn't show (being a black-and-white photo) all the flowers that were most certainly here at the time of the battle. June is when the prairies really fly their colors, the month most prairie wildflower species bloom. Now, in late May, the early-season flowers were just coming into their own. Some native, some introduced.

Introduced? That's right. Even though the Little Bighorn Battlefield has never been turned by a plow. Even though the grassland has not been grazed in over 116 years. Even though the Indian victory has been honored by leaving this patch of prairie as the prairie people fought to preserve it, it is not the same prairie. Over time, nonnative grasses, such as bulbous bluegrass and Japanese brome, and nonnative wildflowers, such as goatsbeard and Canadian thistle, have taken root beside native species, such as blue grama and globe mallow. If you were to ask the person in charge of maintaining the battlefield's historic vegetative integrity, she'd probably tell you that the Battle of the Little Bighorn never truly ended. The contest between natives and nonnatives for control of the prairies continues today.

But on June 25, 1876, day one of the battle, all the grasses and all the prairie flowers would have been, like the seven thousand Sioux, Cheyenne, and Arapaho peoples gathered on the far side of the river, native. It was the men of Custer's Seventh Cavalry that constituted the invaders.

Sitting at the base of the monument, hearing the angry hum of the weed whacker that had replaced the roar of the leaf blowers, I tried to envision the sound and fury that must have ensued when 839 well-armed cavalrymen and officers went head-to-head with 1,500 highly motivated and battle-hardened warriors. It was an epic and hard-fought battle involving brave fighters on both sides, and it was also, as concerns the prairies, pivotal.

And maybe it was because I was having trouble hearing birds over the racket. And maybe it was because, as most visitors who come to historic places do, I was trying to find commonality with the past. But I found myself wondering whether the meadowlarks and grasshopper sparrows and other prairie birds continued to go about the business of being birds during the battle, or whether they were forced to quit the field. There would have been young birds in nests, in June. The battle raged for three hours. That's a long time to neglect nestlings, who must be fed almost continuously during daylight hours and protected from the sun. The parents, I think, would have been as motivated to attend to the needs of their young as the Sioux and Cheyenne and Arapaho warriors were motivated to protect the people of their villages.

And I found myself wondering, too, whether it would have made a difference in the outcome of the battle if Custer had had a small battery of leaf blowers under his command. Firearms the Plains Indians understood and used with skill (as the white marble markers scattered across the prairie attest). But a device that roars like an inestimable swarm of really pissed off bees and is able to command the Four Sacred Winds might have been a force that would have sent even the proud Sioux warriors back across the river.

God, I hate leaf blowers. I wish they'd put a bounty on them.

CLASH OF CULTURES

There were more visitors arriving at the monument now. Some were serious history buffs. People who could tell you how many men fell under Reno's command. People who could bring an arsenal of facts to bear when arguing whether Crazy Horse did, or did not, make his epic charge out of the north to overrun Custer's position.

Most were simply tourists doing the circuit. Yesterday they visited Mount Rushmore and squeezed in Devils Tower. Today they were doing the Little Bighorn. Tomorrow, it was on to that park with all the geysers. Jellystone or something.

All who come to this place are fascinated by the heroic stand that was made here. It's part of our psyche. It's part of our heritage. Few probably comprehend or even think of the cultural and historic context of the battle, much less the series of decisions and events that started the pieces moving on a collision course.

You could argue that the conflict began when the disgruntled Sioux, and their allies, ignored the edict made by the Bureau of Indian Affairs for all tribes to return to established reservations by January 31, 1876, or be treated as "hostiles."

You could argue that it began when gold was discovered in the Black Hills, in Sioux territory, in 1874, and the U.S. Army was powerless to prevent hordes of treaty-breaking gold miners from entering.

You could argue that it was nothing more than the continuation of a policy of genocide and usurpation on the part of the American government whose roots go all the way back to Plymouth.

Or, to give this a more positive spin, you could argue that it was just the young United States of America realizing its "Manifest Destiny," which was dominion over all the lands lying between the Atlantic and the Pacific.

While all these things are supportably true, they fail to address the real source of the friction between native peoples and the European invaders. The fact is, you couldn't find two cultures more different in terms of their regard for and treatment of the land. And when you come right down to it, most of the conflicts that have taken place on this planet have been fights over land.

You can call it "territory" or "resources." You can, as many nations do, cloak territorial ambitions in ideological terms. But ultimately, most wars are fought for control over land. In the case of the "Indian Wars," the land was a whole ecological biome. Linked to it was the native peoples' way of life.

European Americans consider land a commodity, something to be used in any fashion that serves interest or need. Their perspective is anchored in an agricultural tradition that goes back eleven to twelve thousand years. It is theologically sanctioned by a Judeo-Christian tradition that gave man dominion over the earth. It received legal and political traction from a group of influential thinkers, most notably John Locke, who postulated that "property" results when the raw material of the natural world is modified by human labor.

It pretty much defined America's attitude and approach toward the prairie, and it made going out onto the prairies and turning over eight thousand years of ecological refinement so you could plant a grain first cultivated in the ancient Middle East right, legal, and proper (in addition to divinely sanctioned). On top of this, you could feed your family and sell the surplus to buy more land, or shoes for the kids, or that fancy new Winchester Model 94 you coveted.

The Plains Indians had no agricultural tradition. They were, like the biblical Abel (the one who was murdered by his farming brother), a nomadic people who were tenders of the herd. They followed the bison. They considered themselves physically and spiritually bound with the prairie and all the creatures that lived there—which, in scientific point of fact, they truly were.

You are what you eat. The trillions of cells in the human body replicate and die as long as we live, and the raw material for those cells comes from what we ingest. If you eat bison, you are only one step removed from feeding directly on grass and two steps away from Mother Earth.

The Plains Indians had no sense of property ownership.

The earth, to the plains people, was their mother. You could not parcel or apportion the earth any more than you could your own mother. Doing so would be akin to destroying the Holy Temple or dismembering and selling off parts of Jesus.

So there you have it. The conflict boiled down to two proud peoples, with diametrically opposed needs and traditions, contesting the same piece of land.

If the Sioux won, they not only maintained their heritage, culture, and identity but saved the biological integrity of the prairies.

If the European invaders won, native culture would disintegrate and the grasslands would be destroyed, but America would become an agricultural giant, feeding its growing population and adding to its overall prosperity.

But very few of the people who come to the Little Bighorn Battlefield care about much beyond the immediate conflict that was the battle itself. A battle that cost the lives of 263 U.S. soldiers, between 40 and 100 Native Americans, and was, at once, not only a resounding victory for the Sioux and their allies but also the last hurrah for their culture—another way of saying it was all downhill from here. Because while the Sioux might have been able to demonstrate their military prowess in a single show of arms, they were, as a culture and a people, unable to win a protracted war of attrition.

One of the advantages of an agricultural society is that it can support and maintain a standing army—professional soldiers whose job is waging war full-time.

One of the disadvantages of a nomadic, hunting society is that young men are hunters first, warriors second. If you are constantly on the warpath, your people don't eat. If you are trying to find and kill dwindling numbers of bison, you have a difficult time defending your borders.

One by one, as the bison diminished and military pressure continued, the tribes gave up their nomadic lives and accepted life on the reservations. By 1881, the age of the free-ranging Plains Indian was over. Deprived of its principal defenders, the days of the native prairie were numbered.

So when somebody asks you what the Battle of the Little Bighorn was really all about, now you know. It wasn't about broken treaties. It wasn't about facing impossible odds. It wasn't about President Ulysses S. Grant versus Chief Sitting Bull or Crazy Horse versus Custer or even the Seventh Cavalry against the Sioux.

It was all about grass, like the stuff lying over and around the graves of the fallen, like the stuff rolling down the hill toward the Little Bighorn. Like the stuff that used to cover nearly one third of North America and whose fate was sealed here. What brave men fought and died for here was grass.

"What are you doing?" a voice I recognized as Linda's asked.

"Watching grass grow. You?"

"Shooting," she replied. "Want to move up the phylogenetic ladder and watch flowers grow for a while?"

"Sure," I said.

We walked down the cinder walkway that leads toward the gully where some unknown number of Custer's troops tried to break free from their encirclement during the last stages of the battle. None survived, not there, not anywhere on the ground held by the troops in Custer's command.

In the tradition of heroic stands, they were killed to the last man. And while the Indians were victorious on this day, on July 25, 1876, a national monument was originally, and perhaps ironically, established to honor the defeated soldiers, not the victorious natives.

But, you might be thinking, the preservation of the native grasslands represents at least a token, maybe even a philosophical victory for the Sioux. Yes, it does! Except for one funny and undermining thing.

You can't walk on the grass at the Little Bighorn Battlefield. All visitors are enjoined to stay on established paths to safeguard the integrity of the battlefield. But if the Sioux had won the war and not just the battle, they probably would not have denied visitors the right to walk across Mother Earth.

GONE TO FLOWERS

The trail, which winds steeply down, cuts through green grass and past small white stones bearing the legend "Unknown Seventh Cavalry Soldier." These are not gravesites per se. The "remains" of the men of the Seventh lie interred in a mass grave beneath the monument atop the hill. The stones mark the spots where the bodies were found and hurriedly buried by their comrades. It was a year later, following reports from passing settlers about the appalling state of the battle site, that remains were gathered and finally laid to rest.

The stones are just historic reminders.

Maybe.

"Know that one?" I asked, pointing toward a patch of ground just off the trail. "The pretty little blue one with the yellow center?"

"Umm, yeah," Linda said. "That's blue-eyed grass. We saw it on the Comanche Grassland, remember?"

"No," I said, and it was true. When it comes to wildflower identification, I'm in a lower decile of my graduating class. Linda's the botanist in the family.

Still, I like plants. The fact that I can't pin a name to a flower doesn't make it any less beautiful, and it doesn't diminish my appreciation by a petal, pistil, or stamen. Besides, I've got Linda when I need an identification.

"How about that one?" I asked, directing my wife's attention toward a cluster of creamy white, tubular blossoms. The plant was everywhere on the battlefield—more common than marble markers.

"That's a locoweed or crazyweed. Don't ask me which species, though."

I didn't ask. I was already distracted by other flowers—and there were many to be distracted by.

Like spiderwort, a beautiful violet-colored blossom with three heart-shaped petals arrayed around a ring of golden-headed stamens. The tentaclelike leaves make the ground-hugging plant look as though it were groping in the air.

And globe mallow. A sweet-scented, coral-colored flower that smells like honey spread thick over bread.

The faces of Custer's men, lying behind the breastwork they made of their fallen mounts, would have been nearly flush with the earth as they struggled to hide from the hail of arrows and bullets arcing toward them. In a lull in the battle, amid the choking smoke and dust, did any expend a portion of the last mortal moments left to them to smell the flowers crushed beneath them?

Did they wonder what species they were? Did they savor their existential beauty? Did any of these young men in their final moments try to hide from the approaching horror behind the memory of honey, still crunchy in the comb, served up on bread still warm from the oven?

"Here's a new one," Linda said. "Camas. Death flower. Pretty, aren't they?"

"Really pretty," I agreed, looking at the ghostly pale petals that offered no scent. "Why death flower?"

"All parts poisonous," she said, quoting from scripture (the plant field guide).

"Well, if it was known that an emissary of death was this attractive, bodies would be lining up," I said, realizing that here, in a national cemetery, such was the case.

"Sorry," I said to the nearest headstone. "But you'd really like this flower. Even if you've seen it before."

And I'm sure he would have, whoever the fallen soldier was. Very few people will tell you that they don't like flowers—in fact, I'm not sure I've ever met one. Such being the case, there are few places on the planet where a person who likes flowers would rather be planted than the prairies.

Long before ecologists talked about the water cycle, long before scientists broke the code to the citric acid cycle, the Plains Indians recognized that there was a cycle to life. It was at once very personal, because it was the story of each individual's own life, from beginning to end, and universal, because it engaged and involved all living things, which excludes little under the sun. To native people, wind was living, water was living, and, of course and especially, the earth was living. It was not called "Mother" for nothing.

And what the native people knew all along, we understand and are coming to respect today. The earth is living, in both a holistic and a literal sense. Exhume a shovelful of prairie soil and you unearth millions and perhaps trillions of microscopic organisms, all living lives as worthy of that label as you and I. In this sheltered underworld, these microorganisms go about the business of living and replicating, as all living things do, and part of their daily routine involves breaking down nutrients, locked up in dead plant and animal matter, that they then return to the soil to be taken up in the roots of plants that have the power to restore these particles of matter to life! Putting the recycled essence of once living, now dormant things back in the game, where they may become part of a stem, a petal, a stamen, or a grain of pollen that might be carried, by butterfly courier, to another flower nearby.

Or the flower might be eaten! By a prairie dog or bison.

The prairie dog might then be killed by a swift fox. Who then carries the life-giving package back to her pups, who use much of it in their effort to become big foxes (and return some of it to the soil on a recycling fast track called defecation).

And when the young fox who, with luck, becomes an adult fox finally reaches the end of his or her own personal cycle and dies? What happens to all that life-sustaining stuff that's been temporarily stockpiled in the form of a fox?

I think you know the answer, and I'm sure you've also guessed where this line of thinking is going. Because most of the remains of the young soldier whose commemorative stone stands on the Little Bighorn Battlefield are not entombed in a deep, anaerobic sepulcher atop the hill. Nor, in fact, do they lie intact near the stone. In the days, weeks, and months following the battle, most if not all of the bodies of the fallen soldiers were almost certainly exhumed by four-legged scavengers. The remains were partially consumed and scattered. Insects and the small microscopic emissaries of decomposition went to work on what matter remained.

The prairies in 1876 were still roamed by wolves, bears, coyotes, badgers, and other assorted meat-eating animals. The shallow graves in which the bodies of Custer's men were laid offered scant protection, and some of the fallen were merely covered by clods of sod.

So most of the remains of Custer and his men stayed close to where they fell, where in various ways, over the course of four seasons, they were returned to the cycle of life. Only bones, for the most part, found their way into graves.

Part of us recoils at the thought of the bodies of brave young men, killed in the spring of their lives, denied a decent burial in the Christian and European tradition. But it may help to know that the native peoples harbored no such misgivings and held to no such tradition. The warriors killed at the Little Bighorn were removed after the battle and their bodies placed on raised scaffolds to hasten, not deny, their return to the cycle of life. In the tradition of the braves they fought, the soldiers who died on the prairie very quickly became part of the prairie, where they were taken up by other living things. Transformed into bears and badgers and grasses and . . .

Flowers! Like the ones poking up through the prairie landscape, then and now. Able to respond, as living things do, to the warmth of sun, the touch of rain, and the brush of wind.

Able to be admired. By two visitors from New Jersey. One a writer, one a photographer. Who are at some unknown point in their own cycle of life but who are, now, able to experience the warmth of the sun, the touch of wind, and the great peace and unifying commonality that battles confer upon a place.

In the end, no matter whose side you fought on, no matter what party you voted for, no matter how high you sit upon the trophic ladder, you are only one step removed from Mother Earth, in whose embrace we become one.

"How about this one?" I asked, indicating a big, showy,

yellow flower with a sunburst array of petals bisected by dark, radiating spokes. It looked like a fireworks display on a stick. It was the flower closest to the stone marking the location of the nearest unknown fallen soldier.

"Goatsbeard," Linda said. "It's an Old World species. Nonnative."

"That's perfect," I said.

"How so?"

"It's thematically apt. Did you know that 44 percent of the men who served under Custer were foreign born? Mostly Irish and German. Odds are pretty good that there's a little bit of Hans or Paddy bound up in that flower. Did you get a picture of it?"

"No," she said. "It's too far from the path."

We walked to the end of the trail, then back. There were flowers and stones all along the route. One animate, one not, both paying tribute to the same thing.

In time, we returned to the van and started south. Memorial Day weekend was almost upon us. We wanted to be off before the hordes hit the highways. Our destination? Back one more time to the place where the story began.

Like the seasons, we'd come full circle.

CHAPTER 12

Crow Valley, Pawnee Grassland, Colorado

ON THE ALMOST-SUMMER SIDE OF LIFE

Jupiter was still visible as I stepped away from the van, sunrise still a good forty minutes off. Arcturus, the brightest star in the summer sky, was low in the west. Known to the Lakota Sioux as Itkob u, "going toward," it was also called Ihuku Kigle, "it went under." The reference, I learned, is to the birds that migrate north in the spring. I've loved this bright orange star for as long as I can remember. Now, I have another reason to favor it.

Meanwhile, here on planet Earth, the day was mostly about breeding birds, not migrants. Early as it was, the predawn mutterings of western kingbirds were climbing to a squealing crescendo. To the west, the local great horned owl was saying both good morning and good night.

Probably the same bird we heard back in February, I thought. The kingbirds, of course, hadn't been here then.

Or the western meadowlarks and American robins that greeted us when we'd stopped here, briefly, in late March.

Or the brown thrashers, which arrived about the time we did earlier in May.

Or the western wood-pewees and common night-hawks that had just arrived in the last couple of days, rounding out the roster of Crow Valley breeding birds.

Now they were all present and accounted for. All the birds of a prairie summer were finally here.

Out on the grasslands, things were waking up, too, but here in the campground, over the din of robins, several dozen campers were still sleeping the good sleep of people whose real-life cares are still one third of a three-day holiday weekend away.

Except for Linda, of course, who was only half asleep and busy getting the dogs and the van ready for travel. This was the morning we'd been dreading—one of those days in the far distant future that you think will never arrive. This was the preordained last day of our prairie spring. We were going to catch the morning light, do a little photography, then hit the road.

Our adventure was over. Arcturus, the Summer Star, said so.

It's not that there wasn't more to discover, more elements to the prairie spring that we would have loved to engage and to share in these pages. There certainly was! But spring isn't just a phoenix. Spring is a chimera, and an elusive one at that.

While we were here, spring was also happening over there. When we went there, we discovered that the season had already jumped two squares ahead or had danced two steps to the side or had treacherously doubled back, and now we were missing some fantastic spectacle right where we'd been.

But isn't this always the way it is with spring? Always seems to happen just when your back is turned. Except now the season wasn't behind us. It was racing ahead. Already way up north, where spring is more a timid visitor than a full-fledged resident.

Meanwhile, here on the prairies, the season had all but passed us by.

You're shaking your head no. I know what you're thinking, and I know what the calendar says. Spring, according to the angle of the sun, the orbit of the planet, and the *Farmer's Almanac*, runs until June 21. You think we're selling the season short.

Sorry. We're not. Not here. Not at this latitude. Not in the lives of wild things, which are the only arbiters with standing. If you were to look across the prairies now, you'd find that breeding territories have already been established, mates wooed and won; trees were in full leaf, dozens of species of flowers already up; and the animals that emerged to see their shadows back in the early days of spring (which are also the late days of winter) are chasing them now, doing their best to hold the frantic pace that summer levies against all adult things.

If you were to go out on the prairies now, you'd find young longspurs and meadowlarks crowding one another out of nests. For some species, like American robins and horned larks, first broods would already be on the wing. With apologies and understanding (because don't we all try to make spring last beyond its natural limits?), I have to tell you that young birds in nests and fledglings on the wing are elements of summer. They do not fit into the template that is spring.

Spring is the time of becoming. Summer is the busy time of being. And summer, my springtime friend, is a whole 'nuther season; a whole 'nuther book. It has come time for this one to end.

I walked across the grass, heading for the open country beyond the trees, avoiding the gravel drive, preferring wet sneakers to waking campers. It was getting light, quickly, and by the time I cleared the trees, it was light enough to see the white ovals on the wings of the common nighthawks crisscrossing the sky. Light enough to see my frosted breath, the only vestige of winter that still survived. Light enough, by the time I reached open prairie, to see my shadow reaching out and across the landscape, almost, but not quite, touching the horizon.

At 5:38 A.M., a strong, summer sun—just as strong as the sun is in late July—broke into view and very quickly, very literally, took my breath away. The warming rays swept the chill from the air and the last vestige of winter with it. There was no longer room or reason for spring now. Summer had come to the prairies, and it was here to stay.

For as long as seasons last.

As I started my return, I reflected back. Upon the four-month project that had allowed us to experience so much but had had, at its onset, no more substance than the shadow that, on February 2, we flew all the way out here to see. And I couldn't help but think how much a person's life is like a shadow.

When we are young, standing tall as we can in the morning light, it stretches out in front of us, pointing the way toward possibilities that seem beyond reach. At noon, with the sun high above and life at its pinnacle, our shadow disappears, we think, or maybe we're just too busy to notice it. Later, as evening gathers and we have time to reflect and more to reflect upon, we look back over our shoulder, and there it is again! Falling along the path we've taken and, if we are lucky, upon many wonderful experiences extending all the way back to . . .

Well, I think I'll leave it to you to fill in the blank. You have your shadow. I have mine. And for a time, as the story of our prairie spring unfolded, your shadow and mine walked in lockstep. Writing, as I love to point out, is 50 percent reader. As people and prairie have become inseparable, readers and writers are one. For as long as stories last.

But you'll have to excuse me now. As a naturalist and a writer, I have dutifully and happily shared our adventures with you. If you've forgotten, just look back. Books have a lot in common with shadows, too.

There are only a few hours remaining now, and I find at this late date that I am reluctant to retire this project and to surrender my own tenuous hold on spring. So, if you don't mind, I'd like to excuse myself and keep what little is left of the season to myself.

Make that ourselves. Because I can see Linda standing in front of the van now.

She's pointing at her watch.

She's waving me to hurry.

I didn't realize that I'd walked so long, that the sun had climbed so high.

Damn.

We're wasting good light.

Bibliography

Brock, Jim P., and Kenn Kaufman. *Butterflies of North America.* Boston: Houghton Mifflin Company, 2003.

Comanche National Grassland. U.S. Department of Agriculture, Forest Service, 1999.

Egan, Timothy. *The Worst Hard Time.* Boston: Houghton Mifflin Company, 2006.

Goodman, Ronald. *Lakota Star Knowledge.* Mission, S.D.: Sinte Gleska University, 1992.

Groundhog Day. Stormfax Weather Almanac. www.stormfax.com.

Groundhog Day. Wikipedia, the Free Encyclopedia. http://en.wikipedia.org.

Johnsgard, Paul A. *The Prairie Dog Empire.* Lincoln: University of Nebraska Press, 2005.

Jones, Stephen R., and Ruth Carol Cushman. *The North American Prairie.* Boston: Houghton Mifflin Company, 2004.

Kays, Roland W., and Don E. Wilson. *Mammals of North America*. Princeton: Princeton University Press, 2002.

Little Bighorn Battlefield. U.S. Department of the Interior, National Park Service, 2002.

McGaa, Ed. *Mother Earth Spirituality*. New York: Harper-Collins, 1990.

Michno, Gregory F. *Lakota Noon—The Indian Narrative of Custer's Defeat*. Missoula: Mountain Press Publishing Co., 1997.

Moul, Francis. *The National Grasslands*. Lincoln: University of Nebraska Press, 2006.

Pawnee National Grassland. U.S. Department of Agriculture, Forest Service, 1999.

Pollan, Michael. *The Omnivore's Dilemma*. New York: Penguin Press, 2006.

Reish, Edward C., Virginia Downing, and Thomas Nidey. *Lamar, Colorado—Its First Hundred Years*. Lamar, Colo., 1986.

Rey, H. A. *The Stars—A New Way to See Them*. Boston: Houghton Mifflin Company, 1952.

Savage, Candace. *Prairie: A Natural History*. Vancouver: Greystone Books, 2004.

Spellenberg, Richard. *National Audubon Society Field Guide to Wildflowers*, western ed. New York: Alfred A. Knopf, 1979.

Stebbins, Robert C. *Western Reptiles and Amphibians*. Boston: Houghton Mifflin Company, 1985.

Strahler, Arthur N. *Physical Geography.* New York: John Wiley and Sons, 1951.

Strickler, Dee. *Prairie Wildflowers.* Columbia Falls, Mont.: Flower Press, 1986.

Van Bruggen, Theodore. *Wildflowers, Grasses, and Other Plants of the Northern Plains and Black Hills.* Interior, S.D.: Badlands Natural History Association, 1971.

Venning, Frank D., and Manabu C. Saito. *Wildflowers of North America.* New York: St. Martin's Press, 1984.

Williamson, Jack. *Wonder's Child: My Life in Science Fiction.* Dallas: Bendella Books, 2005.